CALUMET COLLEGE
WHITING, INDIANA

Business

and

Social Progress

Business and Social Progress

Views of Two Generations of Executives

Clarence C. Walton
Contributing Editor

PRAEGER PUBLISHERS
New York • Washington • London

PRAEGER PUBLISHERS
111 Fourth Avenue, New York, N.Y. 10003, U.S.A.
5, Cromwell Place, London S.W. 7, England

Published in the United States of America in 1970
by Praeger Publishers, Inc.

Library of Congress Catalog Card Number: 78-104393

ACKNOWLEDGMENT: The preparation of this book was aided by grants from the JDR 3rd Fund and The Fund for Adult Education.

Printed in the United States of America

Editor's Preface

The increasing social involvement of American business under the impact of dynamic and widespread change, the various forms this involvement may take, and its effect on the traditional structure of the corporation were foremost in the thinking of the Committee for Economic Development when it set about organizing the series of discussions that form the core of this volume.

These discussions were unusual both for the time they spanned and the numbers of people involved. Over the course of nearly a year, CED sponsored five regional meetings at which more than a thousand younger executives of business organizations examined the corporate responses to the new challenges in roundtable sessions under the guidance of deans of business schools. There was no effort to arrive at a consensus; the purpose of these discussions was to stimulate individual thinking in a setting of free debate characteristic of CED's proceedings since its founding in 1942.

At the conclusion of each meeting, a panel of CED trustees selected from among the participants those who had made an outstanding presentation of their individual viewpoints; five of these younger executives were then invited to present their views at a national symposium on "The Future Role of the American Corporation" in New York City before an audience of trustees, advisors, and guests. Distinguished commentators, chosen from among the ranks of the older generation of leaders in the business and academic communities, entered into a dialogue with the younger generation of executives. To give broader perspective to these discussions, at a later meeting ten of the founders of CED reflected on the major social and economic developments that have occurred in the past twenty-five years and that are likely to occur in the next quarter of a century.

These meetings were CED's way of marking its twenty-fifth anniversary. However, it was not the historic nature of the event but rather its forward thrust—the concentration on the next quarter of a century—that gave it significance. That and the opportunity afforded both younger businessmen and their elders to pause at a significant moment in national and world history to see where the road has led and where it may be leading. The forward thrust is reflected in this volume of papers resulting from the meetings.

The book is divided into three sections, the first of which comprises the dialogue between the two generations of leaders that took place at the symposium,* augmented by two papers of particular interest. A prologue by Alfred C. Neal, President of CED, sets the stage for the ensuing discussion. This paper is an extension of remarks written by Neal for an ongoing CED study concerning the structure and performance of the corporation. The second paper, by William C. Stolk, Chairman of CED who was also the chairman of the anniversary program, examines the possibilities of restructuring corporate management so that social involvement can become an integral part of corporate function. This paper is a fitting epilogue since it comprises Stolk's reflections on this topic in the light of his many years' experience as a business leader.

The second section of the book is devoted to the reflections by CED's founders on the nature of the vast social and economic changes that have occurred over the past twenty-five years and on the unfinished business that remains for CED and the corporate world in the coming years. This material is significant not only because of the ideas it expresses but also because of the authors, who played important roles in the shaping of American society during the mid-twentieth century. These papers have given the editor an opportunity to comment on the role of business leadership over this period as seen in terms of CED's contribution in modifying conventional business and economic philosophies.

In the final section, the editor has attempted to place the entire CED proceedings and the reflections of both the younger and older generations into a larger historical framework. In doing this, I have drawn on and elaborated ideas and concepts developed over a number of years in writing and teaching about business responsibility and economic history.

Finally, I would like to express my appreciation to the trustees and staff of CED for their very useful suggestions, comments, and editorial assistance.

Clarence C. Walton
Dean, School of General Studies
Columbia University

---

*ACKNOWLEDGMENT. The remarks by these ten participants (pages 25-32, 35-41, 43-48, 51-57, 59-65), as well as the remarks by Emilio G. Collado (pages 9-10), are reprinted with the permission of the *Saturday Review.*

Contents

Business

and

Social Progress

Introduction

The Corporation and the Institutional Crisis

CLARENCE C. WALTON

Within the American business community, the large and established corporations are being urgently summoned to tackle problems that under a normal profit-and-loss calculus appear often as only marginally related to economic matters. Indeed the problems appear more meta-economic in character as one considers such things as pollution, deteriorating public schools, the financial plight of private colleges, the psychology of the hard-core unemployed, and health services for the indigent. Representing areas for potential business response, all these fall within the rubric of "corporate social responsibilities."

In surveying this *terra incognita* there is a powerful impulse to reckon with the costs of corporate involvement. Can an enterprise provide a satisfactory return to its stockholders, pay adequate wages to employees, and maintain a competitive position in the market when it seeks to train people who may be ill-prepared and ill-motivated toward work? Does it make sense to "give" substantial sums to universities—only to learn that the gifts fall far short of the institution's needs? Can any large enterprise literally "afford" to release top officials for heavy involvement in university and in civic affairs? The fact is that with increasing frequency, corporations are answering these questions affirmatively.

There was a time when business decision-making, according

to the traditional theory of the firm, was reduced to a simple formula; namely, the rational selection of alternate courses of action in order to maximize profit. There was a time, too, in our history when belief in inevitable progress—especially among the middle-class—was taken more as an article of faith than the rival Calvinistic doctrine of a fixed universe.

More sophisticated analysis, however, indicates that rationality in decision-making does not always and necessarily imply profit-maximization; traditional theories fail to explain the diversity of business behavior and tend to break down when confronted with other motives. Profit, therefore, becomes one element for business decision-makers and this element must be set within the context of others, including the psychological satisfactions sought by senior decision-makers, the departmental and personal objectives of subordinates, and the firm's conception of its social responsibilities.[1]

Clearly business leadership has a profound role in the furtherance of social progress. Historically that role was presumed to be filled by strict adherence by business to its economic functions narrowly conceived. In the contemporary setting the business role has been extended to relate to social activities indirectly dependent on the economic performance and even to noneconomic endeavors. Often this new role is described in terms of a corporation's social responsibility. But tracing the erratic evolution of the term "business social responsibility" in this country—so loosely handled in theory and so differently embraced in practice—leads to generalizations having more exceptions than are found in French grammar. The concept's content frequently seems less determined by logic, fact, or even changing circumstances, and more by those whose voices are heard in the semantic wilderness.

The historical meaning of business responsibility runs a wide gamut. At one extreme the emphasis is on strict attention to owner claims to maximum profit on investment, with employees, customers, suppliers, and the public at large viewed as *outsiders.*

This interpretation has been variously labelled. It has been called by Richard Eells of Columbia University the "austere" model of enterprise and by Francis Sutton of Harvard University the "classical" version of business philosophy. At the other extreme the stress is on balancing the rightful interests of all claimants, including society at large. This more recent and clearly broader view of corporate responsibility has sometimes been called the "metro" model of corporate activity by some and the "managerial" philosophy by others.[2]

Between the two poles are many variations on the theme because special needs and special circumstances often suggest to management that one of the claimants should be accorded primacy over others. Enterprises therefore can have various goals, and in meeting them it is quite possible for a company to be responsive and responsible in one area at the same time that it is unresponsive toward other societal needs. A company may, for instance, provide high wages and good working conditons for employees while withholding corporate support for local tax programs designed to improve a rundown school system. As any survey of corporate behavior will reveal, it is the well-established and mature enterprise, such as found among *Fortune*'s 500, that realistically can be expected to be the pace-setter in discharging certain responsibilities toward endeavors not directly linked to the enterprise's normal functions.

Basically what is occurring today is a rising social challenge that requires business to move beyond the austere model and to espouse a managerial philosophy which takes explicitly into account the special needs of the public interest. Placed under severe and critical analysis is the traditional doctrine that "what is good for business is good for the country" and the related premise that business fulfills its complete responsibility when it achieves the maximum output of goods and services. While material abundance is obviously a primary measurement, it is now suggested that business has the capacity to influence many other things essential to social progress—the rate of economic growth, the economic base of the educational system, the nature of work and its related consequence on family life, plus others. This has introduced a new element that must become part of the corporate structure.

Leaders of private corporations are actively seeking new ways to effectuate the kinds of changes that are implied by the new societal requirements. Corporate leaders increasingly recognize that while Americans continue to want the material goods of life, they also want to achieve the good life. Assumed is corporate efficiency; *demanded* is corporate equity. Put briefly, equity in this context means sharing in the obligation to build a better America according to the extent of the corporation's human and financial resources.

In the CED-sponsored dialogue between senior and junior executives, articulate representatives of two generations of businessmen, having peered into a full-length corporate mirror, present a rather unanimous report. What is seen is a vigorous and muscular business enterprise system, justly proud of its enormous economic achievements. Surrounding it, however, are stunted social realities in the form of ghetto slums, urban sprawl, obsolete schools, racial tensions, and the like.

To the critical businessman the sight stimulates a resolution to respond constructively; to the critic of business the scene is obscene. The contrast between those hostile to the business community and those committed to it might be expressed through homely analogies. Often critics of business view society as a seesaw; if only the high side (business) could be lowered, the depressed side (society) would automatically rise. Executives, on the other hand, too often perceive society as a kind of jet plane where differences exist between first-class and coach but where the passengers all ride at the same speed, at the same height, and to the same destination. As thus seen by some businessmen, those who still lack resources to travel on the space ship of American prosperity can be expected to take a trip later —if properly prepared for it.

It is this ignored stratum of American society that increasingly commands the attentions of business managers. A century ago the frontiers for business were unused land and untapped resources; today the frontier is the city and all that it represents. And having been spectacularly successful in the use of human talent for the direction of physical resources to predetermined goals of production and distribution, corporate executives are convinced that their proven skills can be constructively applied to today's social ills. There is increasing understanding that anything done to raise the economic level of the poor, the intellectual level of minority groups, and housing accommodations in the slums will redound to the good both of the society and of the business community. Failure to respond can only mean a steady corrosion of the quality of American life.

What emerges as the business "case" in the presentations of those who participated in the CED forum is based on an acute awareness that contemporary society is marked by change, confusion, confrontation, and crisis.

Change, which came historically from growth in population and growth in nature's productivity, often abetted by the factory, now comes from a science-related technology. And yet the true genius of the nation is seen less in its scientific breakthroughs than in its entrepreneurial capacity to market new products emerging from scientific research. The differences between continental and American businessmen is instructive. Cryogenics, laser technology, basic advances in holography, fluidics, and the office-copying-machine industry were all European in origin, but their markets are found in this country. Theodore Levitt of the Harvard Business School summarized the matter in these words: "It is the great entrepreneurial energy, managerial effort, and involved preoccupation with the consumer's motivations and need that distinguishes American . . . business enterprise."[3]

There is an obverse side to the coin. To the assumption that technology is good because it induces growth and productivity is added the further assumption that growth itself is good. According to the American gospel, growth reflects the dynamism of an achieving society, and achievement always means social progress. To be bigger *is* to be better. Today a different message is being urged upon us. Increasingly questioned is the easy identification of growth with progress. Countries (and cities within countries) view with apprehension the influx of people to their borders; colleges set limits on enrollment and expansion; businesses grow bigger but lawmakers frown. When, for example, the electric power industry responded to public demands for more energy by announcing a 6 to 7 per cent increase annually in production, vociferous complaints were quickly heard regarding the dangers of thermal pollution and other problems. Recently the distinguished editor of *Science*, Philip H. Abelson, editorialized on the problem of "the inexorable exponential" this way:

> Society has been, and still is, on a great growth kick. If we are interested in a long-term future for man, we will regard rapid growth with suspicion. We will look for, and point out, the unexpected and unpleasant consequences of exuberance long-continued, and seek to moderate it before irreparable damage has been done.[4]

Barbara Ward put the matter more on personal terms when she noted the limits on an individual's capacity to consume beyond the "fourth car, the third swimming pool, the second house"; to her the great need was to recognize the simple fact that enormous increases in productivity will surge forward in the face of desperate failures by the market of humanity and the market of mankind to expand at the same pace.[5] It is only natural that if business has received major credit for the nation's past growth—and hence its progress—it should now receive some of the blame from those who are concerned by the dislocations caused by technological developments. As one executive has remarked, our very living habits "are changed by the endless flow of innovations from our research-minded corporations. The natural environment is affected, and the man-made environment is largely created, by the actions of the five million firms that make up the American business community."[6]

Because ours is a world of accelerating changes, a lively scramble goes on constantly within business to identify those important "turning points" which provide clues to the future and, by clear implication, challenges to the present. The reason for this diligent—sometimes even frenzied—search for meanings that will bring conceptual order from institutional disarray lies in what one scholar has called a "moral crisis in management."[7] It is a crisis precisely because business leadership has not yet found a satisfactory basis for articulating its basic beliefs and the corporation's primary purposes at a time when the rationale behind the old profit ethic—which in its simplest form states that managers are beholden only to stockholders—seems woefully deficient. Indeed, one of the most revealing commentaries on the shift of emphasis was made fifteen years ago by Adolf A. Berle, Jr., one of the most perceptive analysts of the corporate scene:

> Twenty years ago, the writer had a controversy with the late Professor E. Merrick Dodd of the Harvard Law School. The writer (Berle) holding that corporate powers were powers in trust for shareholders while Professor Dodd argued that these powers were held in trust for the entire community. The argument has been settled (at least for the time being) in favor of Professor Dodd's contention.[8]

In a real sense the argument is only partially settled. For if the number of constituents with valid claims on the corporation has been enlarged, it is still a matter of debate how the priority of claims should be established, what price stockholders should be asked to pay when management responds to other claimants, and how conflicts of claims should be resolved.

What is becoming painfully clear is the fact that institutional adjustments to change are under increasing stress. Technological change proceeds with a geometric progression whereas institutional and individual change moves at an arithmetically progressive rate. Hence the distance between change and adjustment tends to widen despite heroic attempts to cope with the events. As the gap increases, spontaneous groupings spring up to create "confrontations," and we witness confrontation by police and firemen's organizations, by teachers' unions, by community association, and, of course, by students. Unhappily, the "confronters" often embark on courses of action which are deliberately designed to make rational discourse impossible; the excitement of the event seems more important than the meaningful participation in the process of reform.

What often happens is that the response is inadequate and that the confrontations increase in number and intensity. Resort to violence, which was once thought to be the possession of the unskilled working classes, has now become a property of the black minority, the activist collegians, and professional white collar workers. Except for the Civil War, the capacity of our political system to contain violence has never been more challenged; except for the great depression, the will of the business and other parts of "the establishment" to meet social needs has never been more questioned.

The New Deal has come and gone. The Fair Deal has come and gone. But for many the Great Society has not departed because it has never arrived. Few people employ the words of these slogans, which today in utterance seem too biting, in discourse too shallow, in content too superficial. How can one explain the demise of a noble slogan? A ready answer is that all rhetoric of a "great" society creates ambitions too high and expectations too unreal for early fulfillment. Another response would take into account the present world situation from a larger perspective. Historian Fritz Stern has indicated that the thirty-year period between 1914 and 1945 constituted a disaster period which must be viewed as a unified epoch—not unlike the period encompassed by the famous Thirty Years' War (1618-48) of three centuries ago.[9] At that time European states fought a titanic struggle the end of which marked a great *caesura* in western history. Feudalism had died; Christianity was sundered; the age of faith had yielded to an age of reason.

So too, is the fact that our own epoch marks a great *caesura* in the western world. With the end of World War II, the U.S. and the U.S.S.R. emerged as superpowers; England no longer ruled the seas; parochialism was replaced by cosmopolitanism. Our epoch has been marked by a wide margin for novelty expressed by such terms as the "new economics," the "new morality," and the "new business." In each case the precise meaning of the term still eludes us, but the future general directions are certainly becoming more sharply etched for business as corporations accept a greater social role for the over-all health of American life and for the quality of our civilization.

Participants in the CED symposium explicitly recognized the historic nature of the present moment and have implied that it is a transitional stage for the corporate community. Of interest are the remarks by Emilio G. Collado, Chairman of the CED Research and Policy Committee, in summing up the dialogue between the junior and senior generations of executives. One of the critical problems noted by Collado is how the search for purpose can be carried out and translated into a meaningful organizational setting. He puts the issues in these words:

> It seems to me that three main propositions have come out of this symposium.
>
> The first is that American business will have to do a good deal more to help solve the nation's social problems. The younger business executives clearly feel—and our CED commentators concur—that the corporation as such should identify those social problems on which its particular resources and skills can be most effectively brought to bear and make these virtually as much a part of its business objectives as traditional commercial activities.
>
> The second proposition is that we are not quite sure how to carry out this new business commitment to social problem-

solving. Both generations of business executives agree that the profit motive is the key to any substantial application of corporate resources. There is a general feeling, too, that to a much greater extent social problems could somehow be converted into profit opportunities in the best sense of the term. This may be easier in some areas than in others.

Now, I do not propose to be the first chairman of a CED Research and Policy Committee to preside over the liquidation of the profit motive—and in any event I do not think I could get the committee to adopt the proposition—but it strikes me that we may need to re-examine our traditional concepts and measurement of "profit" in this context. For example, substantially greater corporate financial support for education, all things considered, may result in greater profits within a reasonable payout period.

Required, too, is a completely different kind of business structure, and a completely different set of standards for measuring performance would be required for corporations to attain the objective of dual service to shareholders and to society. . . . But so far we really have not developed anything like a clear corporate rationale and strategy for this task. This is going to require a good deal more work.

The third proposition that came through these discussions is that business and government will have to develop the same kind of effective partnership in social problem-solving that has hitherto only been achieved in major wartime emergencies. . . .

A final point should be made about the language employed by both generations of executives. Interestingly enough, there is little use by the authors of these papers of the older traditional terms to describe the nature of the contemporary business system. "Administrative economy," "laboristic society," "free-enterprise system" and even "mixed economy" appeared rarely if ever, but the desire for a new term that is descriptively accurate and normatively acceptable is palpably present.[10] What was rarely said but clearly implied was this message of great importance; namely, that the corporation has been enormously successful within its sphere even as other institutions have been less successful in theirs. There is, in short, an institutional crisis in the country and corporate leaders are groping, sometimes unsurely, to determine more precisely what areas can most effectively respond to intervention by the corporation.

The nature of the institutional crisis is important for businessmen to grasp; only through such understanding can business leadership grapple with the implications of an important conclusion. Put simply, the conclusion is that other institutions, which often established, inculcated, and monitored values and value-acceptance, are themselves in great crisis. As a result the business community is increasingly being asked to generate a new set of values—a new ideology—that makes sense both to business and to the society of which it is a part.

rarely said but clearly implied was the message of great impor-

[illegible]

PART ONE

The Corporate Response to the New Challenges

1. Fundamental Issues in Business Structure and Performance

ALFRED C. NEAL

The preponderance of private production of goods and services in the American economy is carried on by large publicly owned corporations. The 500 largest corporations account for two-thirds of the assets of the nonfarm economy and more than one-half of all U.S. manufacturing and mining company sales. There are good reasons for the predominance of the large firm. Consumers tend to prefer their product, perhaps because price and quality reflect the economies of scale that large corporations make possible. Government depends upon them to perform essential national functions—developing and making weapons systems, correcting the balance of payments, alleviating the ills of the cities. A large proportion of young people starting their careers choose in favor of the large corporation, and most will never know any other type of employer. Investors in great numbers prefer their shares to those of smaller enterprises. Yet, despite its important place in American economic life, the large corporation has attained at best only an ambivalent position in American economic thought.

By and large, professional economic thought about the corporation, competition, the organization of the economy, and public policy toward the private sector is premised upon the development and refinement of the doctrines of Adam Smith and his successors in British and American economic thought. There is ample material already available describing this system of thought; we need no more than sketch an outline to recall its familiar major principles.

Each individual and firm if left alone will normally seek its maximum advantage. For the firm to seek maximum advantage means to seek to maximize profits. The fundamental drive in this system, therefore, is selfish interest. Pursuit of selfish interest is checked and guided by competition. In other words, the opportunities of firms or individuals to extract excessive profits or remuneration are brought under control by competition. As Adam Smith said, each individual left to pursue his own selfish interest is guided "as by an unseen hand" to promote the public good. A corollary of this view of the role of competition as it applies to labor is that unions are basically monopolistic and possibly destructive of the self-regulating nature of the system. Moreover, since the firm is supposed to maximize its profits, there is a constraint on philanthropy by the firm; it has nothing to give away because profits are the minimum required to stay in business.

The role of the state in this system is well circumscribed. It is to provide peace, justice, police, and a few other essentials. The modern day extension of this limited role of the state as it applies to the private sector is that it should promote the conditions of competition; i.e., it should see to it that no firm or organization becomes so large or so powerful that it succeeds in insulating itself from the forces of competition in the market.

It is worth noting in passing that the essentials of this system of thought were developed before the modern corporation emerged as an important force in the economic life of modern nations. Smith's own view of the corporation of his day was that for want of incentive to be efficient, it could perform only routine functions requiring very large capital, such as building and operating canals and waterworks.

It would be a travesty to consider modern economic thought to be limited to the concepts just outlined. The separation of ownership from management in the corporation has had extensive treatment. The social responsibilities of companies have been recognized and a rationale for "corporate philanthropy" developed and is to some extent practiced. A role of unions different from that stated above has long been argued by labor economists and recognized in law. Most of all, the limited role of the state envisaged in the Smithian system has long since given way to a concept of the state as politically responsive, interventionist, and welfare-conscious. Nevertheless, the main stream of thought with respect to the nature of the firm, its motivations, and the desirability of competition as a regulator has remained basic in the thinking of most economists. They have either insisted on the need to break up large firms to achieve competition or have re-defined "competition" to accommodate firms of the size we have. Economists, in one way or another, have learned to live with the conflict between ideology and fact. And for much of economic activity carried on by numerous small-scale producers, there is little conflict between ideology and the facts. This paper is not concerned with that part of the economy.

For those whose immunity to schizophrenia is low, this state of thought has led to a search for an internally consistent alternative that might envisage a set of forces influencing large corporations to function in ways which would produce social results comparable to those claimed for laissez-faire. In the next few paragraphs I shall try to outline the hypotheses on which an alternative *non-dirigiste* intellectual system might rest. Most of the papers that are included in this book either assume or are in search of such a system.

In the new alternative model, we start with the world as it is. We recognize the corporation as the dominant form of organization in our society and the large corporation organized for profit as being responsible for a major part of the gross national product. We recognize that management in the large modern corporation is separated from ownership and has tended to become increasingly professionalized. We recognize that ownership of the large corporation has come to be concentrated in institutions that are motivated to hold or sell on the basis of market performance of their holdings, with the possibility of wide divergences between corporate performance and the market performance of their shares. We recognize further that the corporation is essentially a political institution, whatever its economic objectives may be.

As a professionally managed political institution, the corporation could not possibly be guided by a single goal such as the maximization of profits. A political institution must obtain the consent of the governed. The consents that are needed are diverse and vary from institution to institution. In the case of the corporations, the groups from which consents must be sought include management, stockholders, the work force (with perhaps several different strata), customers, suppliers, bankers, and financiers. Likewise included are local communities in which there are important plants or offices and often the governments of several countries, as well as the various levels of government that are often customers, regulators, and lawmakers—and in all instances, tax gatherers.

Managements of modern corporations may not like or even appreciate the role assigned to them in this alternative system as governors of political institutions. Probably three-quarters of the speeches and writings of corporate managers contain some complaint about "government interference." This is some evidence that the people running one form of government recognize the threat from another form. Because of the intellectual support that management can derive from Adam Smith's "free enterprise" thinking, management usually bases its case upon a set of ideas which, oddly enough, are also used by others to support the antitrust policies management finds objectionable. This fact makes it very difficult for us to get over the first hurdle standing in the way of accepting a new set of ideas. That hurdle is recognition of the modern national publicly-owned corporation for what it is—essentially a form of government which happens to be devoted to pursuing some goals that are different from those of political government, but also some that are the same. The similarities, incidentally, give rise to well supported efforts to make government more "businesslike."

If the modern corporation is a multi-goal interest-balancing political institution, what are the limits to its power? How can we be sure that the exercise of its political power does not bring to the participants in it—either stockholders, management, labor, or some other group—rewards out of proportion to contributions? How can we be sure that its pursuit of its own goals will bring it to pursue the public interest? As the power of the large corporation grows, how can we avoid a clash between it and the political governments which have authority over it? How can we be sure that the political governments, seeing themselves outflanked by economic giants, do not enter into alliances with giant corporations to compromise goals of both, thereby producing results that are less than those most preferred by the public constituencies which they share?

Our hypotheses about the nature of the corporation must go beyond those so far stated. We must also develop hypotheses about how socially desirable results can be anticipated and measured for large national publicly-owned multi-goal organizations having considerable market and political power. Ultimately, we must form a judgment about whether corporate aberrations from socially desirable behavior will be self-correcting or will require corrective intervention by others, and if such intervention is required, whether it should be *ad hoc* or by changes in the rules applicable to all.

We can begin by insisting that every corporation, like every government, can define its goals. This is a view consistent with good management principles, and it seems reasonable that corporations can not only formulate a set of broad corporate goals, but that these goals could be generally acceptable.

It seems inconceivable to me that any set of corporate goals could for long be out of harmony with the socially desirable goals acceptable to government and to the people generally. Goals would include self-preservation and growth through the production of goods and services that people want and are willing to pay for, and that by and large would yield a profit. They would include returns to stockholders adequate to attract capital and retain stability in management. They would include rewards to labor that would attract a sufficient labor force of the required training and skills, and provide scope for growth and creativity for individual members of it. I could extend this list but the work already done in this field is extensive.

If the line of reasoning is acceptable so far, we encounter our first major empty space. There is little in the accounting and reporting systems of corporations that would enable us to determine either whether corporate managements have well-formulated sets of goals (other than those put out by the public relations department) or to measure the extent to which in any given period of time goals have been used as guidelines for operations or that progress has been made in a consistent manner toward a realization of the goals guiding company policy.

As Rensis Likert[11] has pointed out, present corporate reporting permits management for a considerable period of time to present glowing results in financial statements at the expense of consumption of human capital—in management, in work force or in customer and public good will. This great gap in the reporting system of corporations—particularly of the large national publicly-owned corporations—cannot long remain unfilled. Demands for better "social performance" call for goal setting and performance measurement. It is worth a major effort to explore the possibilities of filling the gap. A viable alternative to an enforced return to laissez-faire or to a highly interventionist state depends upon development of a reporting system for large corporations that discloses social as well as financial performance.

Once the gap in the reporting system is filled, then possibly a real alternative can be developed. That alternative might follow these lines: Managements of large publicly-owned national corporations, as governors of political institutions responsive to and dependent on a consent of the governed, have limited discretion. They must formulate socially acceptable corporate goals. They must balance interests and particularly the interests of the consumer and of government in pursuing their goals. Operating in a goldfish bowl of reporting progress toward goals, if they veer too far in pursuit of one to satisfy its interest at the expense of another, they will be brought into check by the powers that can be exerted by those whose interests are slighted. For example, if the stockholders are being given undue rewards, the pressures arising from the side of labor, either organized or unorganized, and from potential competitors, will tend to restrain management's lurch in the wrong direction.

If, because of union pressure or just plain bad bargaining, the rewards to labor become substantially larger than are necessary to attract and motivate an adequate labor force, then pressures from competitors, consumers, and stockholders can be expected to be exerted to restrain this aberration. Government, too, may play a role; e.g., by insisting on open unions in the highly paid tightly organized industries.

If the company gets too cozy with government at the expense of the interests of stockholders, labor, or customers, or any combination of other interests, pressures can be expected to come from the interest groups slighted. Government arm-twisting of corporate executives can go only so far in depriving others of rewards that might be theirs.

It should be noted in passing that the concept of the corporation—its interests and the way in which those interests can be harmonized, if not optimized—permits fulfillment of a wide range of social responsibilities. The company's objectives include its "public business" as well as its profit-making objectives realizable by the sale of goods and services. Clearly the corporation has objectives beyond those that can be met through the market.

William C. Stolk's paper in this collection develops both the concept of "public business" and the way in which it can be organized. A company's objectives with respect to labor, for example, may involve extensive educational activities not directly related to the operation of the company but related to the company's need for talent in the future; it needs to be attractive to certain types of graduates of professional schools, etc.

The concepts of "public business" and "multiple goals" relieve —if they do not cure—the schizophrenia of the classical Smithians. The financial rate of return need not be the same on all lines of a company's business, as is implied by profit maximizing. Financially, some lines may turn in a loss that represents in reality an investment in personnel or market development which has a high payoff in the future. Other financially profitable lines, by achieving profits at the cost of destroying human capital, may be reducing the company's future profitability significantly. Lending executives to government—certainly not a costless operation to a company—may well pay off in the development of government approaches that lead to remunerative "public business" later on. While considerations of this type may not have the determinateness of a mathematical formulation, they do emphasize that there is more to management than can be found in the text books. A computer can maximize profits; only good management can operate a company to optimize the achievement of multiple goals.

We now arrive at the ultimate hypothesis, which is more a question than it is a hypothesis. In the Smithian system, it was the unseen hand that was counted on to lead the pursuit of selfish private interest into realization of the public good. In the alternative system suggested here, it is the *visible hand* that is expected to achieve the same result. Our problem is to find out *whether the hand can be made visible,* and having been made visible, *whether it might be expected to guide the corporation to optimize the results for all of those having a reasonable interest in its operations.*

There will be no simple formulas that can be used to determine whether a company has optimized its results but one can conceive that a good deal of computer activity might be employed to measure comparative performance of various companies in the pursuit of their various stated goals. With or without computers, an adequate scheme of performance reporting will permit shortcomings to be detected if the system gets out of whack in one company or another. The power of comparison in the hands of intelligent analysts is enormous. Aberrations from desirable behavior are likely to set some equilibrating forces in motion. Can we identify those forces, and can we have some assurances that they will work in the not-too-long run? A major challenge facing business, government, and scholarship alike is to develop a system which measures the extent to which companies make progress toward meeting all their important goals. The papers contributed by the younger executives move us a long way toward identifying those goals. Beyond measurement but more challenging would be the appraisal of how corporate goals relate to the goals of society, and how changes in one affect changes in the other. Examination of that area will inevitably bring to business and to government tools of analysis which will contribute greatly toward an allocation of resources in keeping with the more efficient pursuit of the public good.

2. Reconciling the Conflicts of Plural Goals

Sensitive awareness of the high stakes of failure in an age of increasing social dynamism permeates the following comments by Robert J. Weston and the critique by Raymon H. Mulford. The former concentrates on the need for organizational changes to accommodate the young people flowing into managerial positions; the latter emphasizes the necessity for a new statement of corporate principles.

Weston is concerned with this "critical" generation of young people under twenty-five and the critical questions they ask. They ask not to be treated as numbers, occupants in an organization chart, or pills in a box, but as human beings with personal needs and ideals. Above all, it is quite clear that our traditional views of authority—as we have known them for almost 2,000 years—is not being listened to by youth. One management consultant, J. Clayton Lafferty, has said that in ten years corporations will probably not be able to operate a company in which the employees are not heavily involved themselves in making decisions that affect them.[12] To these "new" men and their needs Weston directs his remarks. It is his basic conclusion that the organization must respond to people who wish to make a contribution to society, and he implies that unless the corporation is restructured to accommodate not only these new men but the new plural goals, it is doomed to failure in the convulsive years ahead.

Casual observation confirms the dangers that are implicit in this warning. Contemporary society stresses property rights less and personal rights more. The "outcasts" of society are claiming, as personal rights, access to decent housing and jobs, good schools and hospitals, open opportunities for political involvement in society and, especially, opportunities for retrieval if failure attends the initial effort. L. W. Moore recently observed that business must become involved because it is the ultimate source of these. "In the vernacular of the inner-city streets," said Moore, "businessmen are the cats with the bread."[13]

Awareness of these developments prompts Mulford to record in his commentary the conviction that corporations desperately need a more developed rationale to explain the business role in social problem areas. The work of creating the material basis upon which rests other institutions of our civilization is, as Mulford indicates, the work of a creative minority. To him the corporation's interest goes beyond the tensions represented by competing claims from stockholders and from society respectively; rather it is the mature enterprise dedicated pluralistically to a wide variety of claimants—workers, customers, vendors, government, communities, and other less easily identifiable publics. Central to Mulford's concern is therefore the articulation of a corporate philosophy that will bring these functions and interconnections into focus.

Without any doubt, such an articulation is greatly needed, the more so as the older classical explanations of business behavior have been undercut by new conditions and forces. As society increasingly employs different "mixes" of public and private powers to social problem-solving, it becomes even more important for business to explain more clearly what it is doing and why it is doing it. Robert Lilley, President of New Jersey Bell Telephone Company observed recently:

> This "mix" conforms to no ideology or dogma. In the best American tradition, it is a uniquely pragmatic way to get things done. . . . The relationship of the corporation to society is not one we can define strictly in commercial terms. The corporation is so deeply rooted in American life that its relationship to the society that supports it must be defined in terms that are personal, philosophical, and political, as well as commercial.[14]

The implications involved in basing a rationale for the corporation on "personal, philosophical, and political" aspects, rather than solely those of profit-making, are obviously enormous.

Making a Place for Tomorrow's Managers

ROBERT J. WESTON

The future role of the American corporation will involve fulfillment of shareholder expectations and will also involve shaping the environment in which society, as well as business, operates. This is a pluralistic goal. It means serving the owners of the business with profits while serving the needs of people through social progress. If businesses do not take an active role in the design of their operating environments, they will be leaving their eventual destiny to outside forces. To abandon responsibility for the progress of society is therefore the same as abandoning responsibility for the future of the shareholders. This could imply the eventual abandonment of the responsibilities of management.

Not being able morally or financially to avoid this responsibility, the future manager faces critical choices in the performance of his task. He will be expected to manage in two areas that are often in direct conflict, since what is best for the shareholder may not be best for society and what is best for society may not be best for the shareholder. How will tomorrow's manager resolve this conflict? Here are some of the choices he can make:

- He can compromise by moving down a middle road, accepting a little lower price/earnings ratio and turning his public relations people loose on reasonably "safe" social issues. This man will eventually lose his job because he has done neither function particularly well.

- He can turn his entire organization over to an attack on the problems of pollution, birth control, civil rights, and the welfare of the needy. This man must concurrently begin preparing a resumé because he will be out of a job within six months.

- He can totally ignore the needs of society, squeeze harder for reduced costs and higher selling prices, and pay large salaries to young men who will turn gray at an early age. This manager can hang onto his job for quite awhile, but he will leave a mess for the son who eventually takes over the business.

- He can identify needs in the future marketplace that offer opportunities for business profit and identify needs in society that offer opportunities for service to society, then vigorously pursue *both* goals.

If we accept the last option as the logical one, some pressing questions come immediately to mind. How would people in the front office react? What kind of organization would it require to implement the policies that are implicit in this approach? And most importantly, what would the new perspective mean to the company itself? There is little point, of course, in exploring the answers to the second two questions unless we know the answer to the first one. Here we can take considerable hope that Robert Hilbert, First Vice President of the Federal Reserve Bank of Philadelphia, was right when he told the national Conference on Social Welfare in June, 1966, that "social responsibility is *in* and the business 'in-groups' are composed of men who are deeply concerned about social responsibility." If this is so—and the available evidence seems to suggest that it is—the real problem therefore consists in turning the ideology into meaningful responses involving reassessment of corporate purposes and appropriate organizational mechanisms to implement policy.

If we accept the validity of pluralistic goals for the American corporation, then the structure and performance of businesses will change right along with the change in business goals. This will require new ways of organizing ourselves to get the job done, new ways to measure performance of our people and our organizations to make sure that the job is being done properly.

I have yet to see an organization chart that shows *how* the job gets done. Most charts merely indicate that people have protective boxes around themselves. Or they show who approves whose expense accounts. These things are probably necessary for personnel directors, new employees, and an occasional security analyst; they will probably continue to exist. But in truth it must be said that present organization charts just have too many defects. They do not indicate the significance of the white spaces between boxes; they do not delineate lateral communications; they establish artificial management levels; and they imply that an organization is a nonchanging thing.

An organization operates within some scope, some restraints. This could perhaps be represented by the glass walls of a large tank. An organization is not square or round, it is three dimensional; and it is constantly changing all three of its dimensions. This means the walls of this tank must be made of infinitely flexible glass. We look through this glass into a clear fluid, and some place we find a man who manages the organization. He is represented by a floating object. The size of this object, its speed, its shape, its color, its location in the tank—all this depends entirely on the organization under examination. It will depend on a number of variables: the capabilities and personality of the top manager; the placement, size, speed, shape, and color of all the other objects in the tank; the viscosity of the fluid in which they are floating; the month, week, day, and even the hour that the examination is being made.

If such a fluid organizational model were mechanically possible, an interesting phenomenon might take place: each manager in a given company could take a separate, flexible glass tank and graphically demonstrate his own concept of the organization at any given point in time. On comparing tanks, managers would find not the slightest similarities, because this kind of an organization depends almost entirely on the eye of the beholder. It is suggested, therefore, that until some remarkable technological breakthrough occurs in the flexible glass tank industry, and until the day arrives when a hundred managers can sit down and agree on the same organizational concept within these tanks, we do not take organization charts too seriously.

Moreover, the kind of new people American business will need to help accomplish its pluralistic goals just will not fit in the format of today's chart. Some 50 per cent of all Americans are now under 25 years of age, and from this group will come tomorrow's managers of business. Whereas most executives today like pretty much the same kinds of things that their fathers liked, for half the population this may no longer be true. This new generation has been called all kinds of things, but I like best "the critical generation." There are bright young men graduating right now from our colleges and universities across the land who question the way we are doing things. What was good for grandpa is probably suspect, if for the only reason that, it *was* good for grandpa.

These bright young men are going into public service, into research, into teaching, and they are staying away from business careers in embarrassingly large numbers. Yet with our pluralistic, corporate goals of the future, business cannot afford *not* to make room for—and actively solicit help from—these young critics. They are liable to rock boats, ask embarrassing questions, reject company policy, and not understand the meaning of "proper" channels. They will be difficult to manage—but exciting to lead. They must be given assignments that are important to *them,* and then somehow they must be measured and rewarded for performance within the scope of these assignments. They may wear funny neckties and play guitars at lunch, but they are capable of helping us in our pursuit of a pluralistic goal.

Not all the imagination and all the excitement is going to come from the new generation, of course. There is an ample supply of older fellows around just loaded with imaginative ideas and creative designs for implementing them. They may wear funny neckties, too, except they have matured successfully in a more disciplined age.

This, then, is fluid management. It has a minimum of restraints and a maximum of acceptance of its objectives by the people within it. It will be difficult to implement because it has a tendency to destroy artificial status. It removes any opportunity for lethargy. And it requires the ability to create and accept change. This is most certainly not a comfortable situation.

Only as an organization is structured can it perform; only as corporate objectives are identified can performance be evaluated. We all understand financial risk, and modern evaluation technology has greatly increased the odds that our financial decisions will be good ones. So the financial risk here is not nearly as significant as the risk we must take to attract, challenge, and retain bright "fluid" men or the risk we run of losing some previously valuable men in the process. But whatever these risks may be, let us not take the easy way and create "service-to-society departments," thereby establishing isolation wards for members of this critical generation. These people must somehow be brought into all levels of our organizations and given important things to do. They cannot be regarded as threats to the men who approve their expense accounts; we cannot hold their hands and keep them from making mistakes; it will be difficult to motivate them, measure their performance, and properly reward them.

In sum, corporations must look toward the establishment of dual goals implied by the need to serve both shareholders and society. Measuring the performance in achieving these goals will require a completely different kind of business structure and a completely different set of standards, and these will be different for each company because the goals or objectives for each company differ. Boat-rockers, people not in love with the status quo, critics of the establishment will need to be brought into this new structure and then be rewarded separately and identifiably for service to the shareholder and for service to society. For those few people who now have the courage to pioneer this, it will be a tough and frustrating process. But one thing must be borne in mind: it is tomorrow's imperative.

Articulating a Corporate Philosophy

RAYMON H. MULFORD

Robert Weston has truly identified some sensitive and vulnerable aspects of corporate management. However, while he has not gone far enough in some phases of his analysis, he has gone too far in others. He defines, for example, the pluralistic problem of management as balancing the conflicting demands of stockholders for more profits and society for more services. I wish the problem were that simple. In truth, we have the problem of reconciling the demands of employees for more wages, customers for lower prices and greater values, vendors for higher prices, government for more taxes, stockholders for higher dividends and greater capital appreciation—all within a framework that will be constructive and acceptable to society.

Coping with pluralistic objectives, most of which are conflicting, has indeed become the *sine qua non* of industrial management. Most of us have learned that attempting to shift the fruits of our efforts between the various claimants is a self-defeating process. The only answer seems to be to improve our productivity—to expand the total values we produce so there will be more to share with all factions. We will never satisfy them, but our constant striving to do so may constitute our greatest contribution to society as a whole.

Weston suggests that we modify our structures and our bases of motivation so as to attract more of the innovative types and present a brighter picture to the public at large. (As a glass manufacturer, incidentally, I find much merit in his glass tank concept, but unfortunately the flexible glass tank will not be available until the early 1970's.) Undoubtedly we can and should improve our methodology. I believe we have a far more imminent and important job, however. Simply stated, this is to conceptualize the philosophy which underlines our enterprise system in a manner understandable to the general public and to articulate this philosophy to society at large—especially to the academic, religious, and political segments of society. Business is understandable but not understood, and therein lies the danger of restrictions, regulations, and interference that could critically damage the fantastically productive enterprises we direct.

A subcommittee of CED is attempting to come to grips with this problem. While we have by no means reached unanimity on any single aspect, a few basic convictions of some of us may be of interest. In one view, since the corporation derives its legitimacy from the state in terms of articles of incorporation, its basic purpose must be to serve the needs of society through the production of the material wealth required by society. Underlying this is the conviction that our private enterprise, profit-oriented method of operation is by no means a God-given right, but finds its justification in its fantastic success in serving society as contrasted to any other form of economic organization.

Throughout most of recorded history—and throughout too much of the world as we know it today—most of the population has been engaged in laboriously providing the food, clothing, and shelter that are essential to life. It is only when these needs are supplied that any segment of human endeavor and resources can be diverted to pursuits that affect the quality of life rather than its bare existence. In the United States, by contrast, our tremendous productivity, based largely on corporate accomplishment, has enabled a minority of our people to serve the material needs of all of our people, hence our ability to divert the human effort and material resources to build our great educational, medical, political, and other social institutions. If we can articulate the fact that our productive institutions are the foundation on which all of our society rests, it would seem that their nurturing and improvement would be as idealistic a career for our young people as any other.

We must recognize, however, that our very success has created our greatest danger. The majority of our population is not involved in production enterprises, but it has the political power to circumscribe the rules under which we work. Hence my conviction that while we may make evolutionary changes in our structure and attitudes which will be beneficial, our greatest problem is to define a philosophy and to transmit it to the public so that people can make their political judgments from an intelligent frame of reference.

3. Developing Strategies for Equal Opportunity

Experts skilled in the fine art of international diplomacy are forever interested in discovering how the "law of subtle increment" can be used to influence the negotiating process. "Subtle increment" refers here to a willingness by one of the negotiators to place on the agenda an issue previously viewed as nondiscussible. One can note such a subtle increment by Charles Marshall and Philip M. Klutznick, who insist that corporations must be involved in civil rights not only because it is good economically, but because—as Marshall phrases it—"we are big enough to abolish racial discrimination because it is an injustice that we cannot stand to live with in a free society." So stated, the motive becomes one based more on moral than economic considerations.

Probably the different emphasis in the two sets of responses is due to the nature of the problems selected for analysis. Pollution control, for example, is overwhelmingly a technical problem; providing jobs for hardcore unemployables is technical, economic, and social. Why business should be so concerned with the economic side of civil rights requires perspective. With the passage of the Civil Rights Act of 1964, Congress put more legal teeth into civil rights than it had in the ninety years since the Reconstruction. However, instead of disappearing, the so-called "Negro problem" has intensified—clear evidence that black-white relationships have entered a new historic stage.

While Negroes looked first to government for aid, there is now evidence to suggest that the black communities feel both frustration and bitterness over the failure of government programs to make serious dents in poverty, unemployment, and poor housing. The disappointment is sad to record but it has one positive side; namely, a willingness on the part of the blacks to work with the private sector. Important psychological problems, however, must be faced. Three centuries of living in fear of whites, of being exploited by whites and of being taken for granted by whites, have produced understandable antipathies to values extolled by whites. If the whites' "white" problem is racism, the Negroes' "Negro" problem is a loss of a sense of community and loss of individual identity that diminishes the will-to-compete in a white world.

As we now very well know, to help the Negro overcome these psychological handicaps, to recruit and train the so-called hard-core unemployables, to stimulate motivation in people who have been overwhelmed by failure—all this is a tremendous challenge. And it is costly. Furthermore, what makes it difficult for the socially sensitive corporation to move forward rapidly in these areas is the fact that "commitment" is quite uneven between different industries and between different enterprises within the industry. A single company can go it alone for only a measurable distance and a measurable time span. Either the government must change the ground rules to provide new incentives, or a compact among corporations will have to be organized. Perhaps both are needed because the problems are so different. Certainly, as matters now stand, adventurous management must now proceed—as an increasing number of companies are now doing—with a measure of unusual courage in the face of great uncertainty.

Perhaps the world of private enterprise is receiving messages from voices it never really heard before. Twenty-five years ago Langston Hughes wrote:

> Negroes
> Sweet and docile,
> Meek, humble, and kind:
> Beware the day
> They change their mind! [15]

The ominous tone cannot be missed. Yet businessmen can help blacks to "change their mind" only if they change *their* minds. This is the message of Marshall and Klutznick, who thereby give to the debate on corporate social responsibilities a highly significant subtle increment.

Open Doors Are Not Enough

CHARLES MARSHALL

Recently, there was a series of public affairs commercials on television with the theme, "Things Are Changing." They are. One notable change is the attitude of business toward the problem of civil rights. In the long, hard, tedious push to achieve equal opportunity in education, housing, and jobs, business has been a guiding force. But the push has hardly begun.

There are many ways in which business can help. We can open our auditoriums and other facilities for meetings and training. We can give our support and encouragement to our employees' volunteer programs. These things are good, but they are not enough. If jobs are a vital factor in the civil rights struggle—and I believe they are—the responsibility for providing them, particularly for Negro men, rests squarely on the business community.

The government's "war on poverty"—laudable as it may have been—was not even construed by its planners to be an all-out battle to eliminate poverty among the poor whites as well as the poor blacks. In operation, many of the Office of Economic Opportunity programs wound up with less gains to the poor and more to militant power groups. Too often poverty funds become cheap incentives on the market of political patronage. And some southern states refused to take federal money because of a perceived danger to established patterns of segregation.

These observations are not the jibes of an anti-government businessman; rather they represent part of a documented study by a liberal scholar, Ben Seligman. His book *Permanent Poverty: An American Syndrome*[16] makes for dreary reading, particularly his conclusion—and this I cannot accept—that "poverty seems ineradicable." A society as affluent as ours, as inventive as ours, and as moral as ours, cannot forever endure the cancer of poverty in any of its organic parts.

Those of us who have signed the President's Plan for Progress know from hard experience that increasing minority-group employment is not achieved by simply hanging an EQUAL OPPORTUNITY EMPLOYER sign on the door or on every advertisement. It's an important step, already hard won in many firms and necessary in the few whose management remains to be convinced. But it will not generate a flood of minority group applicants. It takes courage and, more important, encouragement to apply today where you were not wanted yesterday—where none of your friends or neighbors ever worked. If the first few applicants are not qualified for any of a dozen reasons, it does not take long for the word to spread quickly that the doors are still closed. This applies of course not only to Negroes, but also to Indians, Mexicans, Asians, and members of other minority groups.

Open doors are not enough. Business leaders must leave their desks and go out and talk to the Negro leaders in their community. Finding them may not be easy. This should not be such a surprise; anyone who has ever tried to set down the names of the leaders of the white community knows the risk of listing "leaders" who talk largely among themselves. Our country is not organized in neat little cadres that follow the lead of ten or twenty spokesmen known to us all. Each block, each street, each corner may have its leaders, its opinion-formers. Some may be full of doubt, cynicism, or even hate. But these are the men who can carry the message to the Negro community. Business leaders must address themselves to these leaders and convince them that their firms are, in fact, looking for their people and trying to hire them.

Today the supply of qualified Negroes is short of our demand. Yet, as we all know, the rate of Negro unemployment in our communities is much higher than average. The explanation lies in the word "qualified." We greet applicants with a variety of tests to screen the qualified from the unqualified. And when anyone questions the accuracy of our tests, we often assume a defensive posture: "They've worked for years—they've given us our present force." Should we not be willing to re-examine the screens we have used in the past? Are we not hiring a man for the balance of his working years rather than for a week or a month? Is it not possible that our tests do a better job of measuring today's ability than tomorrow's potential? Isn't it probably true that the applicant raised in a disadvantaged home tests shorter of his potential than the applicants we have tested in the past?

Many firms are reluctant to hire men qualified only for a job at the lowest level. It is comfortable to have a large number of men obviously capable of advancement. But if we are to employ the lost generations who are unemployed today—many of whom can barely qualify for the lowest-level jobs—we must forego yesterday's policies and learn to work with a smaller margin of promotable employees.

If the tests are worthy of re-examination, so is our training. Much of today's training is geared to equipping the employee for rapid assimilation into the work force. It may not spark the longer leap from stifled ability to total potential required by the minority group applicant. Clearly we may have to use different techniques, possibly take more time, and certainly spend more money to adjust our training to the disadvantaged.

But just filling jobs is not the solution; training is vital to achieving the goal of equal opportunity. The hope the underprivileged bring to that first job will turn into bitterness if we fail to provide for the steady progress of the able. For the Negro's ability to rise to supervisory and management positions is essential if he is to acquire the buying power needed to escape today's ghetto. I do not know whether the mass of Negroes wants to move to integrated housing; you can find leaders to argue either side. But I am sure the ambitious and able Negroes do want to live in the kind of housing to which their improved incomes entitle them. This might be among other equally successful Negroes or in previously segregated communities. But the privilege of making a choice is far too often denied them.

Business is responsible for and capable of making a major improvement in the area of job opportunities. This should not be our total commitment, however. We must apply our power and our dollars in other civil rights areas, too. By this I mean *not* contributing funds to organizations or to facilities that discriminate, *not* locating new plants or expanding present ones in areas that discriminate, *not* selling homes through realtors who block open housing. I hope we will lend our support as individuals and corporations to fair-housing laws. These laws may not solve a community's or a state's problem, but they lay the foundation that is necessary if our Negro employees are going to achieve the equality that most of us already enjoy.

Some of these actions will be hard and will create enemies for us. But I do not believe that corporations today, with the strengths they have now and want to have in the future, can do less than apply their resources, their resourcefulness, and their leadership to a wholehearted endorsement of civil rights.

We must act not because minority groups represent a market or a source of personnel that we need. Not because a solution reached without our involvement could be detrimental to our form of organization. Or not because we cannot afford to abandon the millions of dollars' worth of physical facilities located in cities where the problem is most evident. I like to think we are big enough to abolish racial discrimination because it is an injustice that we cannot stand to live with in a free society.

The Debate Is Over

PHILIP M. KLUTZNICK

Charles Marshall perceptively and forthrightly makes the point that racial discrimination is "an injustice that we cannot live with in a free society," and he urges a speedup in the timetable for "solutions." This is the corporate challenge in today's America.

With notable exceptions, industry and commerce isolated themselves from hard core civil rights issues until recently. There has been an understandable debate in executive suites about the propriety of using officers' time and stockholders' money in this difficult struggle. The shock of a Stokely Carmichael and a Rap Brown and the reaction of vicious and bitter backlash movements, however, have suggested to growing numbers of executives that the very foundations of our free society and abundant economy are under sustained attack. I am not striking a panic button in this evaluation of the basic issue which involves all America, corporate or otherwise. Riots, which ignore the bedrock of democracy—law and order—and gradual solutions which pass over years of discrimination and thoughtlessness, are putting in question our capacity to overcome our domestic ills. This is a crisis which cries out for the best in all of us.

The commendable industry endeavors in the war against poverty, especially in contract operations of job corps training camps; the increasing number of major corporations moving into active job training, job learning, and slum recruitment; the recent business-inspired convening of the Urban Coalition; the tendency to move from token steps to meaningful action—all testify to a remarkable and promising assumption that business and industry are in the forefront of the civil rights movement. This is not an easy road upon which we have embarked, but we must see it through to success.

There is a unique aspect to all this. For years, government, voluntary associations, and labor have been committed to the high ground of nondiscrimination. The promises of a new day have been far more fulsome than the realizations. The gap between reach and reality is still awesome. It is ironic that this period of crisis has emerged from the success of our system, not its failure. As we have attained greater heights of gross national product, the disparity has grown between the 80 per cent who are free and who have opportunities for upward mobility and the 20 per cent who are discriminated against or immobilized. Poverty and discrimination are no longer gray areas—they are black against the background of the great abundance enjoyed by the vast majority.

During the quiet days of the past thirty years when changes in laws and practices gradually emancipated the few, the corporate community enjoyed the luxury of anonymity. Now that prosperity and time have brought an explosion, nearly everyone is turning to commerce and industry to help solve this enormous problem. Indeed, we have a vital stake in it. Without a society resting on law and order and without a willingness to provide for all and serve all without regard to race, creed, or color, we may well have reached our zenith. We could be looking down the long road of decline that has characterized so many civilizations of the past. Many have stumbled on lesser problems.

The debate is over. Increasingly, business must play a leadership role in this disturbing hour. More and more executives are rising to the challenge. There will be no profits and no prosperity if we cannot contain violence while we achieve justice.

There are many indications that leaders of government, labor, and voluntary associations sorely need the invigoration of new recruits from the business community. People who have directed huge enterprises to high levels of accomplishments can bring a new hope and a new tempo to the desperate struggles before us. There *is* an emergency. It must be met with emergency measures. It is time to throw away old rule books and frozen bureaucracies and approach the task with courage and strength, coupled with a willingness to take calculated risks. It is safer to take risks aimed at solving our civil rights problem than to cling to old concepts, looking for a miracle to solve it for us.

Getting into the melee is a risk for business — one that it cannot escape. More will be expected of us than we can produce. But let the best of us do our utmost to cross the treacherous abyss of our domestic turbulence. Corporations insure themselves against all manners of catastrophe; the only true insurance against the ill effects of unsolved civil rights problems is to add corporate capacity and energy to solutions. This is good for our country and good for us. To paraphrase the saying of the sages, though it may not be our lot to solve these problems in the coming generation, it is not our privilege to desist from this work.

4. Applying Resources to Social Problems

Late in his career, Thorstein Veblen, that caustic critic of business, had a sudden ray of hope for the economy's survival when he sensed that engineers were the unsung heroes of the industrial society—the "gifted, trained and experienced technicians" who must rightfully replace businessmen on the "General Staff of the country's industry." If businessmen possess a shrewd eye for the "main chance," namely profit, engineers have a clear eye for the main challenge, which is service. Businessmen are self-serving and engineers are society-serving. In short, engineers would save the country because the business of America was engineering—not business, as Calvin Coolidge said. According to Veblen:

> It follows that the material welfare of all the advanced industrial peoples rests in the hands of these technicians, if they will only see it that way, take counsel together, constitute themselves the self-directing General Staff of the country's industry, and dispense with the interference of the lieutenants of the absentee owners. Already they are strategically in a position to take the lead and impose their own terms of leadership, so soon as they, or a decisive number of them, shall reach a common understanding to that effect and agree on a plan of action.[17]

If Veblen were alive today, it would be interesting to hear his reactions to the thoughts expressed by Henry G. Hohorst and Donald C. Burnham, both of whom are engineers *and* businessmen. These two stress the importance of corporate research and development for social problem-solving—at a profit. Veblen would applaud the former pursuit and condemn the latter unless he saw in the present context the blending of service and profits as clearly as do Hohorst and Burnham.

When Hohorst suggests that turning corporate research and development to social needs means perceptible improvements in the social order and perceptible gains for business, he secures ready assent from Burnham. Of even greater potential importance is the fact that both executives would restrict the government's role to being that essentially of rule-maker and rule-enforcer. Government should develop criteria that provide incentives for profit because without such incentives business is understandably loathe to act.

The importance of corporate research and development to national security and to social progress is properly developed as a major thesis. But present, too, in the remarks is a form of neo-Spencerianism—a thinking that looks askance at government as an "initiator" in our society. The notion of business-government partnerships is carefully eschewed by the authors who make abundantly clear the fact that in their values the private sector is the "activists" in research and development. By expanding the horizons of business, while retaining the privacy of the private motive, the business of America can continue to be business.

The Government's Role: Referee and Rule-Maker

HENRY G. HOHORST

A table fork is an excellent tool for eating. The same fork would be an inadequate tool for digging a ditch. If we are to use the corporation as a tool to help us solve social problems, we must determine what type of tool it is, so that we may use it properly.

What is a corporation? I would define it as a business entity that is designed to provide a service or a product at a profit. The first part is the input; the second part, the output.

In considering input and output, there is a strong temptation for a corporation to siphon off part of its profits to solve social problems. The justification for this approach is to provide an environment that will allow continued profits over the long range. While a definition of a corporation must be built around a long-range goal, we must calculate the price the corporation is paying to provide such an environment. The corporation must also determine if there are ways to provide that environment that more effectively utilize it as a tool.

What about input? What product or services could a corporation provide that would generate a profit and also solve a social problem? Such an approach would cause the corporation to increase its investments and improve its capacity to provide more "social solutions" than it ever could by merely siphoning off a portion of its profits.

What is the role of corporate research and development in determining solutions to social problems? The following are recent examples:

• General Motors Corporation recognized the problem of air pollution caused by automobiles and spent a substantial number of research dollars to develop a device that would help eliminate such pollution.

• United States Gypsum Company recognized the need for improved slum housing and developed a low-cost renovating technique for upgrading more than 300 Harlem apartments. The company plans similar efforts in Cleveland, Chicago, and other cities, and, because of the profit potential, has already invested more than $1,000,000 in such projects. Armstrong Cork Company looks at this profit opportunity similarly.

• Certain railroads recognized that the refuse disposal problem has become extremely acute because of the increasing urban population and the limited landfill sites within an economical transportation range of the major cities. By utilizing their low-cost, long-haul capability, the railroads have developed a waste disposal technique, economically feasible over much greater distances, which permits the utilization of many formerly unreachable landfill sites. A few railroads are also working with major coal companies to utilize abandoned strip mines for landfill sites. This approach will solve two social problems at one time, and in a profitable manner.

In the first example, we find a clearcut case of research used to produce a product that would solve social problems. In the last two examples, in addition to product research there was a significant amount of market and entrepreneurial research to establish the means by which the corporation could contribute to a solution of the social problem.

There is, in addition, a clear demonstration of the need for top-management direction in determining those problems for which we can provide profitable solutions. Without such direction we may find no significant effort being made to determine the conditions or opportunities best suited for corporate participation in social areas.

If this type of research is the job of private industry, what is the job of government? I have often felt that while industry could be considered a player in the game of life, government must be considered the referee and rule-maker. As such, it has no justification for also being the player. However, government does have the right to change the rules of the game—to provide the incentives for the players which will most benefit the community at large.

If we can accept this simplified definition, it becomes clear that government's role is to do research on the problem areas and to evaluate how a change in the rules might provide greater incentives for the players. An example of such an activity would be the approach the state of Virginia has taken to industrial development. Through changes in the state's banking and tax laws, strong incentives have been provided for both communities and private industries to encourage Virginia's industrial development and hence to create many new employment opportunities.

Thus, by utilizing both market research and product research we can tap the profit motive and use the corporation as a tool to solve social problems. History has shown that use of the profit motive is a better alternative for solving such problems than the free use of government largess or the siphoning off of corporate profits.

Growth and Profits Through Social Service

DONALD C. BURNHAM

Henry Hohorst has discussed a subject that is close to my heart, since I am both a corporation executive and an engineer. We in industry recognize the many social problems that face this country and the world, and we are eager to get on with the job. But our motives and our methods should be understood. A corporation cannot justify using the stockholders' money to solve social problems on the slender excuse that this would produce a better climate for profits. Happily, this justification is not needed.

The principal reason industry is ready and eager to work on social problems is that these areas offer great opportunity for growth and profit, as well as for the betterment of our society. Our motives—as they should be in our system of free enterprise—are economic as well as social. The second reason business and industry are eager to attack social problems is that only in this way will such problems be solved. Most of these problems will yield only to research and development by engineers and scientists who are technically equipped to deal with them. Only through research and development can industry provide the greater productivity needed, for example, to solve the problems of the urban ghetto or the underdeveloped nation.

Here is perhaps the greatest social problem of all. The world problem is not underdeveloped countries; it is underproductive people. Only by teaching these people how to produce more and by providing the required tools can we improve their standard of living. That job can best be done by the industrial engineer whose business is improving productivity.

There are other social problems. The food production problem has been solved in this country through a hundred years of research and development in agriculture. In other areas of the world, the solutions must also come through research and development.

Education requires research and development on a concentrated basis, and this requirement is starting to be met. Many companies are now setting up educational divisions or subsidiaries to develop both the "hardware" and the "software" needed to accelerate and expand our educational capabilities. Through new techniques and with computer-assisted instruction, teachers can teach more students more effectively.

Pollution of our atmosphere, once only an annoyance, now ranks as Public Enemy No. 1 in many great cities. No problem facing society cries for more research and development attention than does this. Systems studies of entire airsheds are needed.

There is the problem of fresh water. The needs of our expanding, highly industrialized society are fast outstripping our supplies of usable fresh water. Fortunately, research and development already have scored some important breakthroughs in which government and industry have cooperated. Not long ago, I attended the dedication of a water desalting plant that produces more than 2.6 million gallons of fresh water a day for Key West, Florida. On that day Key West became the first American city to meet its entire water needs through the technology of a water desalting plant—a major social problem solved through research.

You cannot drive into any large city in this nation without being made exasperatingly aware of our transportation problem. It cannot be solved just by building more and wider roads. We must, through research, find new methods of moving people. And that, too, is a job for the engineers of industry, who already are developing some imaginative solutions.

Henry Hohorst asks, "What is the role of government?" I agree with his basic answer, but I would advance his argument even more strongly. Government must certainly guide, encourage, and often sponsor the attack on social problems, but it should leave research and development to private industry, where the forces of competition and the motive of profit will assure the best results.

5. Joining with Government in Saving the Cities

Cities, according to William Dougherty's statement which follows, are in deep trouble, and private enterprise *must* respond because, says Dougherty, it "started the whole mess in the first place." Among the derelictions laid at industry's door are an almost total lack of interest in sound urban planning; a self-serving interest where housing was provided "to keep a captive work force rather than from a desire to cure sociological ills"; and an indifference to the needs of the poor and uneducated migrants who have flooded into urban industrial centers, thus helping to aggravate the social problems that are the deep concern of Marshall and Klutznick.

Starting from this point of view, a very different one from that taken by Hohorst or Burnham, Dougherty quite logically finds that industry now has a moral obligation to mend matters. Nor is it surprising that to accomplish what must be done in the cities, Dougherty likewise finds that "the only sensible solution is a coalition of government and private enterprise," since the problem is too vast for either to handle alone. But realism demands that the profit motive be employed to bring about constructive action. Thus profits *and* morality require corporate responses in the context of the government-business partnership. Commentator James Norton, speaking from the viewpoint of a social scientist, cements this relationship by noting that while both government and business have a distinct role, each is "more dependent on the other than partisans of each like to admit."

That the partnership may be difficult to achieve goes without saying. When it comes to taking the actual plunge into partnership, businessmen are often reluctant and public officials skeptical. One can be sure that where Hohorst and Burnham would prefer government's role to be mainly one of rule-maker and referee, critics of business would answer that business must play a strictly subordinate role in social problem-solving. Michael Harrington has made the "liberal" case against business by arguing that business cannot be relied upon to meet housing needs for families with incomes between four and eight thousand dollars annually.[18] The commercial calculus of land values has already exacerbated the urban crisis and the profit orientation blurs social judgment. (See also Norton's comments along the same lines.) Harrington put the matter bluntly when he said: "Justice is not a sound business investment!"

What is the business response to such criticism? Equality of participation, rather than subordination, appears to be the goal of those who have helped to create such associations as Urban America; the Urban Coalition; the National Alliance of Businessmen; or more recently the Urban Institute, created in April, 1968, by Congress as a nonprofit corporation to serve as a "think tank" for agencies needing research help on urban problems. Instrumentalities for widening and deepening the partnership approach are therefore now in being; what remains to be seen is how effectively they will be utilized by business. Pertinent here in some degree is the question raised by Harrington as to whether "justice is a sound business investment." Dougherty appears to answer this obliquely by saying in effect, yes, if the incentives offered by government are adequate. In replying thus he takes much the same position as Hohorst and Burnham, who likewise see government's role—to their thinking virtually its only role—as offering business adequate incentives for its participation in solving social problems. But with a high degree of realism, Dougherty cites an "added incentive" in warning that "we should keep in mind that if business does not help government solve these problems, government will be forced to go it alone." A very powerful incentive indeed, and one that could alter the usual profit-and-loss calculus of business.

Business' Moral Obligation in Urban Problems

WILLIAM H. DOUGHERTY, Jr.

I am deeply concerned about urban development and the attendant corporate challenge—so concerned, in fact, that my subject could be retitled, "Crisis in the Cities—Help!" Despite suggestions to the contrary, I think the problem of sensible urban development is capable of solution if someone cries "help" long enough and enlightened private enterprise pays heed to the call. It is axiomatic that private enterprise must answer the call, because private enterprise started the whole mess in the first place.

Most of my years have been spent in and around Pittsburgh, the nation's steel capital and a city that has had notable success in solving a critical urban problem. The problems generated by the nation's steel centers, however, have their counterparts in cities served by other basic industries. These industries once required large numbers of unskilled, uneducated, low-income employees to work their factories. Transportation was limited to the railroad or the horse. So the population clustered around the factories and along or near the railroad tracks.

People had to be housed, which meant the construction of many low-priced housing units within the city's core in a relatively short period of time. Because of a lack of qualified city officials to cope with this situation—and a lack of interest on the part of industrial leaders—the uncontrolled growth of this housing was almost completely devoid of sound planning. As a result, no provision was made for highways or for adequate educational plants, parks, and other recreational and cultural facilities. Only a few industries attempted to provide employees with company housing and company stores. And their motives were based largely on a wish to keep a captive work force rather than from a desire to cure sociological ills.

Rapid technological advances and rising labor costs soon began to take their toll on the number of unskilled laborers required in many industries. The result was a higher percentage of unemployment in the uneducated, low-income sector of the labor force. Mother Nature, abetted by masculine virility, compounded the problem by bringing about a population explosion that was concentrated largely in the lower-income urban population. Further complications arose when a breakdown of the sharecropping system in the South sent thousands of low-income Negroes north in search of jobs and nonexistent equality. The outcome was easily predictable. Cities were faced with increased delinquency, a breakdown in the family structure, crime, drug addiction, disease, pollution, and political corruption.

Private enterprise, which started the tragic circle of events, failed to make even a token effort to meet these problems. No efforts were made to retrain those once-productive workers who were bypassed by technological advancement. No efforts were made to control the amount of industrial pollution entering the air and water—pollution which, mingled with that emanating from overcrowded slums and too many automobiles, could bring streams and breezes to the poison point. No efforts were made to alleviate transportation problems created by the heavy urban concentration of people and industry and complicated further by the rapidly increasing number of cars and trucks on too few highways. No efforts were made by private enterprise to solve any of these problems, and therefore the government moved into the picture at local, state, and federal levels. Unfortunately, government was neither adequately prepared nor sufficiently motivated to accept this challenge. The urban problem proliferated.

Those who could afford it took the obvious way out. They moved to the edge of town—and suburbia was born. As the exodus started, the more aggressive retail merchants followed, and thus developed that unique American phenomenon, the shopping center. This co-migration was followed by many small factories whose owners found they could take advantage of suburban facilities with a minimum of capital investment. The middle- and upper-income families, together with retail business and small industry, turned their backs on the city, moved to the suburbs, and pretended that all problems had disappeared.

Ironically, they also began turning their backs on government —at a time when demands on all levels of government were increasing, with a commensurate need for better public servants and greater public support. The core cities were left to decay, and local governmental agencies were left to fight the problems with minimal funds and few dedicated officials. To complicate matters further, Washington began siphoning off the bulk of local tax revenues, a process that returns to the cities much less than has been taken away.

It is painfully clear that private enterprise has a vital interest in solving our urban problems, simply because we bear a large responsibility for creating them. We also have a moral obligation to our communities and our country. I am too much of a realist, however, to think that either of these reasons is sufficient to arouse the nation's business and industrial leaders to instantaneous action. If private enterprise is going to help alleviate the problems, it will take the profit motive to bring it about.

Although many people still think "profit" is a dirty word, it remains the fuel for our economic system. As an added incentive, we should keep in mind that if business does not help government solve these problems, government will be forced to go it alone. When that happens, taxes increase and profits decrease. The only sensible solution is a coalition of government and private enterprise, for the problems are too vast for either to solve alone. The following suggestions show how this joint approach might work.

PLANNING. Initially, government and free enterprise should work together at both local and national levels to identify the problems. Many cities have begun to do this through planning groups and conferences which include business leaders and local government representatives. But they must approach their planning more logically. If systems planning can solve many of our business problems, can it not help redevelop the great cities of our nation? I strongly urge that industry furnish more of its younger, top-flight leaders during the planning phase. Banks, insurance companies, and public utilities—all of which can find a profit motive in urban redevelopment—could take the lead in supplying such men.

HOUSING. Approximately 8 million urban housing units are substandard and must be replaced with adequate housing at a price the tenants can afford. This will require the kind of industrial ingenuity that gave us the low-priced automobile. Local government must cooperate by modifying outdated and obsolete building codes. The federal government should offer business more incentives to invest in our cities—an approach similar to that used in underdeveloped countries. Finally, government-guaranteed credit would enable insurance companies and banks to lend people the money to buy such housing. Recent actions by Metropolitan Life Insurance Company, United States Gypsum Company, and other major companies are good examples of such business-government cooperation.

POLLUTION. Many companies can work the profit motive into solving pollution problems. The Clairton Works of United States Steel Corporation, for example, is recovering numerous chemicals from its smokestacks as part of a pollution abatement process. The profit from the reclaimed chemicals far exceeds that from the sale of coke. The steel industry and many others are now beginning to realize what they can recover from their airborne wastes. In like manner, the pulp and paper industry has created an entire new series of sub-industries based on papermaking by-products that once were channeled off as waste.

It is important that the federal government set pollution-abatement standards—but it is equally important that the federal government provide incentives to encourage industry to eliminate pollution causes. Such incentives could take the form of tax credits or accelerated write-off of capital expenditures.

TRANSPORTATION, EDUCATION, JOBS. A nation that can travel from Earth to Mars should be able to make it possible to travel from one side of a city to another. This is an area in which all the skills and ingenuity of private enterprise can be brought to bear. One prime example is the recent work by Westinghouse Electric Corporation in cooperation with Allegheny County, Pennsylvania, and the federal government in developing a "skybus" transit system for congested urban areas. It is important, too, that private enterprise encourage our school systems to turn out young people who are prepared to make a living in today's world. Our current educational process fails to equip students—noncollege students, particularly—for a productive role in society. Another responsibility of private enterprise is in the employment of slum dwellers. This task would be facilitated by moving more industries back to the cities, and by a vigorous retraining program in the ghettos.

What these examples prove is that something *can* be done in our cities if private enterprise has the will—and the profit motive—to do it. But we have only begun to explore the vast area of cooperation between business and government in urban development. We must find more, faster, better ways to cooperate and conquer our problems—before they conquer us.

Government and Business Are Mutually Dependent

JAMES A. NORTON

Of the signficant phenomena I have observed as a social scientist over the past forty years, one of the most interesting has been the redefinition by an increasing number of American business leaders of the proper concerns of business and private enterprise in areas of public policy. The *involvement* of business leadership in public matters, however, has come slowly to the fore. This is not a moral judgment on motivation. A good case can be made that the singleminded approach to developing our pluralistic, free-enterprise system was necessary to produce an affluent America. The idea that business leadership comes late to public concerns is merely an elaboration of a fact William Dougherty mentioned; i.e., that there have been public costs involved in the earlier business approaches that now rise to haunt us. We have fouled our own nests with air and water pollution, strip mining, and unesthetic physical development, and we must now be concerned.

At the same time that we recognize the propriety—the necessity—of broadened business concerns, we must not replace one extreme with another. We must not now accept the myth that business alone can solve all the problems. Regardless of its talent for innovation and management, business alone cannot rehabilitate substandard housing and provide minimal housing for slum dwellers. There are too many persons whose income could never provide for operating costs, much less for capital requirements. There is virtually no way property can be assembled economically for renewal or redevelopment in most of our central cities, regardless of the skills of the real estate industry.

This example from the field of urban development makes the point that solving public problems demands a partnership between business and government. Each has a vital role that, although distinct, is far more like the other and absolutely more dependent on the other than partisans of either side like to admit. As one who has a foot in both camps, I know that the justified complaints each makes of the other are almost identical. Compare, for example, complaints from the private sector about governmental inefficiency in housing and those made by government representatives citing the languor of Fair Employment companies in increasing their number of minority workers.

Two problems connected with this developing business response to public needs are of particular concern to corporations internally. One is recruiting and developing the sort of young people who can utilize their impressive talents for the redefined goals of the corporation. Some of the seeming disinterest in business of the best students is nothing more than a reflection of the wider range of opportunities offered by a more urbanized and affluent society. Many people agree, however, that more students would be attracted to careers in business if they knew what business really contributes to solving society's problems. It will always be difficult to get this across if business insists that profits alone are the basis for its public concern. There is nothing wrong with honest profits. And there is nothing wrong with honest concern over public needs. But business has not succeeded in properly defining for the outside observer its areas of public responsibility.

The other concern for industry is in developing mechanisms for receiving indicators of social problems as well as for responding to them. This is particularly difficult. Our government is built around such receptors, and yet today it has seemingly been surprised by riots—a rather drastic indicator. Riots have also been an indicator to business, witness the response of Detroit or Cleveland. And some manufacturers now identify Ralph Nader as an indicator of certain social problems. Governmental pressure, too, is gradually escalating as an index of problems such as pollution and unemployment. Clarifying these indicators so that business and government respond in time is certainly a matter of high priority.

All of us are properly proud of the concern and assistance of private enterprise in public problems. It is a particularly American partnership that offers a continuing challenge.

6. Supporting More Balanced Education

The business community has long had an interest, albeit sometimes a narrowly conceived one, in education. That interest has pragmatic roots, a point made by Lawrence A. Cremin of Columbia University in his description of the American attitude toward education: "Education is good economics, sensible politics, and sound defense; it raises character, helps people get ahead; and incidentally keeps them off the labor market for protracted periods of time."[19]

That this pragmatic approach should lead to support for "vocationalism" in the American educational establishment should occasion no surprise. The Morrill Act of 1862 helped to bring into existence institutions designed to train men for effective work on the farms and the land-grant college raised farm work to a professional level. When industrialization intensified the need for skilled workers, and when immigration alone could not supply that need, the country accepted the Smith-Hughes Act of 1917—a piece of legislation where "business influence was decisive."[20]

Over the last half century, and particularly during the past couple of decades, there has been a marked shift in the focus of the business community's interest in education, away from basic vocational training and toward the more professional and scientific aspects of education as represented by the institutions of higher learning. Certainly in terms of financial contributions, corporations have been responsive to the growing financial plight of universities. Corporate grants to higher education have now passed $600 million a year—which is not to say that corporate contributions to higher education are adequate, a point discussed further in the following section of this volume. However, because of the shift of business' interest toward higher education, lower education gets relatively little corporate support. In contrast with the $600 million granted annually to higher education, business gives only an estimated $160 million to primary and secondary schools.

Viewed in this perspective, the comments by Thomas A. Vanderslice and James B. Conant are most interesting. They reveal a desire for a more "balanced" approach by business to the problems of education at all levels. Requested specifically of the business community by Vanderslice is an examination of the critical role of the primary and secondary system. He wants business to support higher wage scales for teachers, and he likewise urges business to support a broadening of the tax base for education in order to provide an equally high level of instruction for all communities, rich and poor. Conant picks up this point in asking for "a radical rethinking of the refinancing" of the public schools; i.e., by the state rather than the local district.

Vanderslice asks for drastic revision of the pattern of vocational and technical education and for active business support in strengthening the entire structure. To Vanderslice's concern with elementary and secondary education, Conant would add a third tier: the community college. "Does not our present pattern," he asks, "which involves a high-prestige value for the bachelor's degree, postpone too long entry into a significant career for many youths?" In effect, both Vanderslice and Conant are suggesting at least a partial return to patterns of business-education relationships that have prevailed historically. They ask business not to forget, in its absorption with higher education, the values of vocationalism which found its most notable expression over a century ago in the Morrill Act.

Broadening the Tax Base

THOMAS A. VANDERSLICE

Most forward-looking corporations have programs for supporting colleges and universities. But very few have considered how they might help our elementary, secondary, and technical and vocational schools. I would like to suggest four forms of assistance which industry is especially capable of providing.

The first is money. Everyone and everything costs more today —teachers, textbooks, bricks, and mortar. Businessmen, including those with small businesses, should face up to what it costs to provide children with an excellent education. And they should be prepared to pay their fair share of the burden. By and large, I believe they *are* prepared, and for very good and selfish reasons. They know that one way to attract and hold the kind of professional management and technical people they need is by assuring them that their children will be enrolled in a good school system.

When a company, particularly a scientifically oriented business, contemplates moving into a community, quite often the decisive factor is not taxes, not the labor supply, and not the nearness to market. What really makes the difference is the quality of the school system through high school. College is not so great a concern, because many children go away to college. It's the local public school situation—kindergarten through twelfth grade—that can determine whether or not a national business will come to or stay in a community.

Business people should, and most of them do, expect to pay for good schools. It makes good lunchtime conversation to gripe about taxes, but our children as well as our businesses derive substantial benefits from the services which tax revenues provide. In fact, we should look with suspicion at any community that offers us too much of a bargain on taxes. I urge that industry support a broadening of the tax base for education. Why should it primarily be on real estate? Why should a community be deprived of a good educational system—and hence of an expanding business base of income—because it is relatively poor?

The second way in which industry can help education is by simply letting the schools know what kind of graduates it can use. I was surprised to learn that we have states whose technical and vocational schools prepare more automobile mechanics than can be employed in a whole region of the country. Another state spends an incredible part of its tax dollars educating farmers when a forecast for that area shows that within ten years the economy will have shifted to an industrial rather than an agricultural base.

It would be a service to business as well as to education if companies informed their states and local school systems about their present and future needs for technicians. Many businessmen would be pleased to be consulted on the content and duration of vocational courses. Too many schools make the vocational course a dumping ground for students with little academic talent. We would like to see young people with technical skills and mechanical aptitude trained to solve the kind of shop and laboratory problems one would actually encounter in industry. But in order to make such training attractive to today's students, business leaders must help to restore to the technician the status, rights, and privileges he once enjoyed.

One problem in education that most businessmen find incomprehensible is the low level of teachers' salaries. This is the third area in which businessmen can lend support. Businessmen, as private citizens if nothing else, must work with school boards, educators, and state authorities to help good teachers to get out of the lock-step salary mediocrity in which they are confined. We should advocate and support a merit approach to teachers' salaries, so that we may encourage those who are better teachers and possibly even discourage those who are more suited for other fields. While our children are graded on ability and effort from "A" to "F," our teachers tend to be rated by seniority. If the merit system were more widely used, the teaching profession would attract more and more of the best talent released by our colleges and universities, and discourage the less qualified. Related to the merit system is the problem of making teachers' salaries attractive to heads of families—specifically to male teachers, who are in great demand at the high school level.

Finally, industry can help educators to utilize the results of the revolution now taking place in information and communications. The last such revolution resulted from the invention of printing, which led to a complete transformation in the way man transmitted his ideas. But although the world of print was ushered in almost five centuries ago, it still dominates our concepts of education. It is a world largely inhabited by those capable of logical, sequential thought generated by impulses received through only one of the senses; i.e., vision. Today, however, we have motion pictures, tape recorders, television, computers, communications satellites—a multimedia world. We have the means to reach an individual through any or all of the senses.

Still, industries that produce this revolutionary hardware are not capable of bringing about the necessary changes without the willingness and cooperation of the educational establishment. New curricula must be devised and subject courses restructured to lend themselves to the media now available. In this era of rapid change, we need a concept of what is possible. I believe that if such a concept is promulgated with the proper genius, we will be confronted by an explosive liberation of human intelligence.

Industry has a tremendous stake in American education. At the same time that we are confronted by an alarming rate of illiteracy—or, even worse, by an alarming number of semi-literates—we are confronted by the discomforting knowledge that we are not challenging and developing many gifted students to full potential. Add to all these factors the shortage of good teachers, the scarcity of money, and the fact that there is so much more to be learned in so few years, and you have a series of powerful imperatives for completely altering the approach to the human learning process.

Working together at this task, businessmen and educators stand to gain much more than they contribute. The synergism of this situation may confound the math teacher, because one plus one in this case will equal more than two. But the public will applaud because it will profit the most.

Why Four Years of College?

JAMES B. CONANT

Thomas Vanderslice has pointed out a number of important ways in which industry can help educational institutions, and vice versa. I am sure all university presidents, either active or in emeritus status as I am, will cheer his opening remarks about money. Certainly the private colleges desperately need increased financial support from companies. Certainly those concerned with publicly supported schools, colleges, and universities must welcome the statement that industry should support a broadening of the tax base for education in the United States.

In commenting on his reference to higher taxes, I cannot resist the temptation to insert a word in favor of a bit of heresy. A year ago, in a second report to interested citizens on the *Comprehensive High School,*[21] I presented data that show the startling lack of equality of educational opportunity between one school district and another. Few people realize the almost accidental way our public schools are financed. Adjacent districts may differ in their taxable resources by several fold. As long as local real estate taxes carry a large share of the cost, such differences are reflected in the expenditures per pupil.

I have slowly arrived at the conclusion that a radical rethinking of the financing of our public elementary and secondary schools is overdue and that in each state the entire financial responsibility should be that of the state and not the local school district. Adopting this unorthodox suggestion would have, of course, as one of its consequences a profound impact on the whole area of teachers' salaries discussed by Vanderslice.

On his second point—the way in which industry can advise state and local school systems about the kind of graduates it can use—I will skip over the vexing but all important question of jobs for the disadvantaged in our large cities and address myself to industry's relation to college students. Today, unlike twenty years ago, the words "college student" do not necessarily mean a youth enrolled in a four-year institution. In many states, the expansion of the local two-year college has been phenomenal. By 1974, nearly a third of all college freshmen will be enrolled in two-year institutions.

Before World War I, many a member of the academic community, professor or administrator, felt impelled to do his or her part to impress on employers the importance of a college education. As a consequence, we find a half century later that the phrases "well educated" and "the holder of a bachelor's degree" are treated as synonymous. Four years' exposure to full-time formal education has come to be accepted by the business community as a prerequisite for many types of employment. This raises an old question: Why four years? Why not two?

I challenge the validity of the widely accepted premise about post-high school education for two reasons. First, because the pattern of public higher education is in process of rapid and drastic change. Secondly, because some, at least, among this college generation are thoroughly dissatisfied with their lot.

Not long ago I attended as a guest—a Rip Van Winkle from the distant past—a series of panel discussions on "Goals for American Higher Education." Two of the speakers represented college student organizations. If their evidence has any validity, they and their contemporaries were far from certain as to why they had entered college. One said that all his contemporaries agreed that the education they were pursuing was "without purpose." Could not such a situation have arisen at least in part because the length of a span of years has come to be the measure of a liberal education? Does not our present pattern, which involves a high-prestige value for the bachelor's degree, postpone too long entry into a significant career for many youths? I suggest that all who are responsible for employment policy consider emphasizing the two-year associate of arts degree and de-emphasizing the bachelor's degree.

I call attention to the role of industry in influencing young people in the community college who have to decide what they should do on completion of the two-year course. The role of guidance and counseling is now shifting from the high school to the community college. The leaders of business can help the two-year colleges by sympathetic understanding and friendly counsel. This is not a new job, but one whose importance gains with every year.

7. Business Involvement in Social Problems: Tokenism or Leadership?

WILLIAM C. STOLK

The development of cohesive and far-reaching public affairs policies and activities by American corporations and business associations is a most important undertaking, both for the future of the business community and for the national interest. President Nixon has emphasized the importance that the new Administration attaches to considerably greater involvement of the private sector, especially American business, in helping solve our country's critical social problems—urban development, civil rights, and education. This is a unique opportunity for the business community to exercise effective leadership. It is also a serious challenge to our will and capacities for asserting such leadership.

Many governmental leaders at all levels, federal, state, and municipal, have increasingly recognized the limitations of public agencies in coping effectively with many of our social problems. These stem from bureaucratic inefficiency and inertia, from inexperience with large economic systems management in nondefense matters, from political influence, and from widespread public resistance to heavier taxation. More and more business leaders are recognizing that the great technological and managerial resources of American corporations are critically needed in the tasks of eliminating poverty, rebuilding the cities, modernizing transportation, cleaning up the atmosphere and water, and bringing blacks and other disadvantaged groups into the mainstream of our economy and democracy.

Both government and business have discovered that most of our persistent social problems are deeply imbedded in the communities where people live and work, that in the final analysis these problems cannot be solved by national fiat but only by community action. Since business is an integral part of the community—it is where we live and work, where we obtain employees and find customers—we have both a responsibility and a self-interest in devoting enough of our resources to help make the environment satisfactory for the citizenry.

We are now very much at the crossroads. If American business in fact undertakes social responsibilities on a major scale, our talent, experience, and resources can provide the critical difference in bringing about a substantial improvement in the environment. If we do not, if we shirk the responsibility or try to get by with public relations gestures and token measures, the country may well sink into chaos, and business will deserve to be discredited.

I want to be quite clear about this. I do not believe that we in the business community have yet given the situation anything like the attention and concentration it requires. I do not think that the evolution of public affairs activities in corporations or business associations, however laudable and promising as initial steps, have yet made anything like the impact that is required even to start getting hold of the problems in front of us. In fact, we are losing ground in many of the critical problem areas—such as the cities—where the deterioration is moving faster than our response, if not our rhetoric.

Let us examine some ways in which corporations can organize and carry out their social responsibilities more effectively.

The first step in my view is for the chief executive officer to establish the corporation's *public business* on the same basis as its *private business*. This means setting up the public business function as a risk-taking, profit-making entrepreneurial operation; not, as is now the case, as a more or less philanthropic activity. I think it has become perfectly clear that anything less than a full-fledged entrepreneurial approach will never engage the serious attention of the corporation and will never make a dent on our social problems.

The *public business* of the corporation must be a *line* not a *staff* function—on exactly the same level as manufacturing and marketing. This completely changes the meaning of corporate execution of its social responsibilities, because it brings these into the mainstream of activity in an organized, systematic employment of resources for satisfactory and profitable performance.

The job of developing and managing the corporation's public business should be assigned to a top executive. He should be an executive vice president because he must function as the chief operating officer for a new and extremely important line of the company's business, with adequate authority and resources to do the job. He should also be a director because the company's public business is sufficiently important to warrant the involvement of the board.

The qualification for outside directors should include knowledge and competence in the broader social, political, and economic affairs that affect the company. Two or three of these directors could constitute a public business committee of the board along with the chief executive officer and our new executive vice president. As a long-time chief executive officer, I am by no means inferring the slightest diminution of the boss's responsibility and authority. I am recognizing the fact that the top man, no matter how versatile and talented, simply cannot give the public business sector the consistent, concentrated direction it must have, any more than he could try to run the manufacturing or marketing activities in addition to his regular duties.

Within the company, the executive vice president for public business must have the corporate resources necessary to do the job. This means *staff*—particularly some of the bright young tigers who are often bottled up in the more rigid line bureaucracies and the idealistic college graduates who have been passing up business for the Peace Corps and the Job Corps. And it means *money*. Since the company has a clear self-interest in improving its social environment, this activity should be considered just as much a part of the true cost of doing business as any other cost—raw material, sales expense, power and light. The monies required should be budgeted and managed as any other operating budget.

Now, how does the new public business department tackle its job? It should start by making an inventory of all the problems and opportunities. One type of problem, for example, is that which the corporation has actually created, such as water pollution. Most corporations now understand that they have the primary responsibility to clean up their own "messes," to use natural resources so as to maintain their value for others.

The opportunities for corporations to apply their resources to help solve broader social problems is less clear, because for the most part these have not been examined imaginatively or systematically. Looked at broadly, there is almost no social task to which all corporations have unique capabilities in research, technology, and managerial skills, and these are precisely what is needed. If Aerojet-General Corporation and North American Rockwell Corporation can apply systems analysis to pollution abatement and public transportation for the state of California, if Eastern Gas and Fuel Associates can build low-rent housing in Boston slums, then every corporation ought to be able to find an area of social improvement matching its capabilities.

After completing the inventory of social problems and opportunities, the public business department should develop a strategic plan. This should take into account: (1) the corporate resources, both money and talent, that would be required; (2) the priorities; (3) the relationship between the company's piece of the problem and the pieces that might be tackled by others in industry as well as by various public agencies; and (4) the results to be attained, both for the corporation and for society. With a strategic plan, a public business budget can be established and operations started, at which point we face three important considerations: profitability, burden-sharing, and the private-public sector relationship.

Of the two ways to deal with the profitability problem, the first is for the corporation to be clear about what it requires to do the job—including tax benefits, specific types of government assistance, or other inducements. The appropriate public authorities can then determine whether the results would be worth the costs, in light of alternative ways of getting the job done.

The second is to re-examine our traditional concepts and measurements of "profit," many of which haven't changed since Adam Smith. We have all heard speeches by heads of companies —I have made some myself—stressing the fact that people are the company's most valuable asset. The speech goes something like this: "We can build factories, build machines and laboratories, but we must have people to manage them profitably." In other words, we capitalize the buildings and machinery, but the crucial human assets of the corporation are not inventoried nearly as carefully as the wood supplies; are not managed with the same kind of cause-effect concern as is applied to the manufacturing process; and don't show up on the balance sheet at all—even though the human assets obviously represent a higher value than all the physical assets.

Our corporations badly need a system of human asset accounting, such as is being developed by Rensis Likert[22] at the University of Michigan, so that we can properly assess the total assets of a business enterprise and determine how well they are being managed. The criterion of earnings per share simply is not adequate because it can and, in some cases does, obscure the underlying reality; namely, that a management is increasing short-run profits at the expense of liquidating human capital.

Once we have placed the proper value on the human assets of the business and their contribution to profitability, we can look at training and educational programs for hardcore unemployables and corporate aid to education in general as *an investment* rather than philanthropy. Better measurements of socioeconomic factors could be achieved through so-called social indicators and accounts, to borrow the economists' terminology. These could enable us to determine with considerable precision the cost-benefit ratio to the corporation of providing special training and education for hardcore unemployables, of establishing businesses in the ghettos, or of making any other investment in the social area. Better measurements would also enable us to determine the broader social effects of such activities, through the reduction of crime and welfare costs, for example, or through the contribution that productively-engaged people can make to their own livelihoods, to their children's educations, and to the increasing prosperity and morale of their own neighborhoods.

In CED we have been working on various aspects of business involvement in social progress for more than a decade, ranging from special programs for distressed areas to education in the ghetto. Most recently, and perhaps most importantly, we have been concentrating on the problem of improving social indicators and accounts so that business and government can develop more adequate measurements for diagnosing complex social phenomena, treating them, and obtaining the desired results. It begins to appear that the social scientists have made enough progress so that an intensified program of business-academic collaboration, perhaps involving government, could produce the kind of specific information that is required by our *public business* department in making its inventory of social problems and opportunities, by business associations in mounting an industrywide attack on problems, and by business and government in determining the most effective allocation of public-private resources to large-scale social jobs.

The second general consideration in developing more effective business leadership for social progress is burden-sharing. As a case in point, industry is spending more than $3 billion a year on air and water pollution abatement, and it is estimated this would have to be increased manyfold to bring the problem under control. Certainly there are very few corporations that would be willing to quadruple their expenditures on pollution control *unless they were sure all their competitors would be just as public spirited.* The result is that business generally proceeds by the lowest common denominator of industry action—or inaction. Government then has to take over and set the standards that industry could have established for itself. Business pays most of the bill—which is almost always higher than if industry had done the job in the first place—and gets the blame for foot-dragging while the government gets the credit for acting in the public interest.

It does not take much intelligence to figure out that this is self-defeating. And it is not too difficult to find a better way. The machinery is already in place in the form of industry or trade associations. What we have to do is turn them around—convert them from rear-guard defenders of the status quo into instrumentalties for collective industry action in the public interest. The industry association is the place where corporate public business executives can bring their proposed action programs, sort out who does what, decide on a fair apportionment of the costs, and work out a detailed industry plan and time schedule for solving the problem. In many cases where industry would act collectively to apportion costs for social improvement, there is no antitrust problem. Where antitrust difficulties may arise because industry proposes to act collectively in developing a new product, government may well decide that the social benefits far outweigh any conflict with the antitrust laws.

I believe this approach has very great possibilities, not just for burden-sharing but more positively for mobilizing effectively the economic resources required to solve major social problems that are too big and costly for any single company. In some areas we are beginning to apply the industrywide approach to the hiring, educating, and training of unemployables. Similarly, corporations in the construction and related industries might jointly supply materials for ghetto rebuilding projects, or for the new low-income housing program, at much lower margins than would be the case in their regular course of business. Most of the major trade associations have done this sort of resource mobilization job in wartime, and the government facilitated it by permitting the lifting of certain peacetime restrictions. There is every reason why we should do the same thing in the comparable kind of national emergency we now face.

The resources are available in the private sector to make the critical contribution to solving our urban, civil rights, and educational problems. Total sales of manufacturing and trading firms, for example, are well over a trillion dollars. Just a small percentage of business gross receipts applied in an organized and equitable fashion to the improvement of our social environment, on top of the present efforts, would make a massive difference without impairing the economic strength of American business in the slightest. And it would be money well invested. It would come back in increasing long-term profitability, in holding down the tax burden, and in assuring an environment for business growth and prosperity.

A final word about the relationship between the private and public sectors. It seems obvious that business and government must develop the same kind of effective partnership in social problem-solving that has been achieved in wartime. This will be helped enormously by business taking the initiative to organize itself for effective action regarding those aspects of the problems it can best handle, by proposing clearly what it needs in the way of reasonable incentives, and by measuring the results of its social investments. We must insist that government do likewise, that it develop an effective organizational structure out of the present hodgepodge of agencies, define its areas of greatest competence, and also measure its results. Government, for example, should pay the bills for general education and other functions of general benefit to the community. And it must maintain the conditions—particularly of high employment and steady growth—under which the private sector can function effectively.

PART TWO

Business Leadership and Public Policy

8. The Attack on Business Orthodoxy

The wheel of leadership revolves rapidly in contemporary society, turnover at the top echelons of the corporate world being fairly brisk. The new breed of managers undoubtedly will bring different perspectives and different visions to their corporation assignments, and in the process they will be led to reappraise critically the judgments of their predecessors. How these appraisals will be concluded a quarter of a century hence becomes a matter for interesting speculation. However, it is worth remembering the particularly apt aphorism that each generation stands on the shoulders of the one preceding it. If the new breed of managers, in making its reappraisal, is able to attain that greater perspective—which allows it to view social and economic problems with both a greater compassion where people are concerned and a greater dispassion where social theories are involved—this will be due in large measure to the efforts of those among the older generation of executives who are represented in the following pages. The young are greatly in debt to these men for having raised the threshold of possibilities available to the contemporary industrial manager.

One can understand the legitimate pride the older men felt in bringing into being an organized and effective challenge to the accumulated wisdom and unassailable orthodoxies that emanated from established business practices and policies. It is clear that their efforts lent strength to the forces working for effective and innovative adjustments by American business. And this revolution, in no inconsiderable part, has been directed against the notion that the particular enterprise is only part of a gigantic economic machine designed exclusively to maximize more and more profit by producing more and more goods and services. There is of course explicit awareness of the importance of efficiency through technological improvements; there is further awareness of the importance of free enterprise in a competitive economy. But there is equally clear recognition of the fact that business policy affects social and political policies, that business acts have social and moral effects.

By holding to the view that planning was both necessary and desirable, this group of men challenged successfully the unwavering commitment of tradition-bound businessmen to the efficacy of an automatically run market system; they preached the heresy that a *balanced* budget was not always a *good* budget; they stated flatly that greater government initiatives were often necessary to the proper functioning of a complex industrial economy; they supported such "socialistic" legislation as Social Security when other business groups fell back; they presumed to ask whether the comfortable adage holding that business should stick to its knitting was not a convenient way to dodge some very serious corporate responsibilities.

William Benton recalls those embattled days by noting wryly how K. T. Keller told the Detroit Economic Club that "the three most dangerous men in America" were Paul Hoffman, Beardsley Ruml, and Eric Johnston. In point of fact these three *were* dangerous in terms of that era's dogmas; others associated with them in CED could be equally included in that classification.

As might be expected, Benton and his colleagues have a vivid sense of history, for they helped shape that history as very active participants. They have held high office in government or international bodies; they have served on commissions or as advisors to government; they have headed foundations, written books, and generally served in the cause of an open society based on personal initiative operating within the framework of public responsibility. Their names in various instances are associated with major social and economic endeavors in our time. This association with momentous events gives them a keen sense both of the continuity of human affairs and of those special discontinuities that work significant watersheds in national development. When they look to the future they tend to see it in terms of the unfinished business in which they themselves were deeply involved—as Paul Hoffman was a moving force in the Marshall Plan, which laid the basis for a new unity of nations yet to be achieved, and as Marion Folsom helped create the social security system, which provided the beginnings of a true social equity in the United States. These men might rightfully be called special pleaders in the public interest.

On this particular occasion, Messrs. Benton *et al.* speak as founders and trustees of CED, with the assigned task of discussing CED's future aims. Hence, their reflections and observations on recent history and the near future naturally tend to be cast in terms of CED's role in events—a role often determined by the force of their individual views.

We Were Once Regarded As Dangerous

WILLIAM BENTON

The future aims of CED are easy to embrace—if difficult to consummate. They are its past and present aims. But, like love, they bear continuous reaffirmation until they are understood. Like the lover, we must proceed on the faith that once understood we shall be irresistible, and being irresistible we shall be accepted.

Fortunately, these aims are today much better understood than they were back in 1942, when secret meetings within the orbit of the Chamber of Commerce in Los Angeles—Paul Hoffman's home town—painted CED's founders as communist-tainted pinks. There was also the occasion on which K. T. Keller, then President of Chrysler Corporation, told the Economic Club of Detroit that the "three most dangerous men in America" were Paul Hoffman, Beardsley Ruml, and Eric Johnston.

When Paul Hoffman and I called on Senator Robert A. Taft in 1942, in our new roles as CED's founding chairman and vice chairman, the Senator scoffed at our arguments that the United

States needed a postwar gross national product of $150 billion to $155 billion to avoid mass unemployment. The Senator told us, "Mr. Alfred Sloan and I have agreed that it is impossible to have a gross national product of over $100 billion." Then he added, "I have the unemployment problem all figured out—just prohibit all women from working." (May I suggest that this may be the key to Paul Hoffman's precipitous dedication to General Eisenhower's Presidential candidacy?)

Now, just what were these original CED aims that were incomprehensible to some and dangerous or disloyal to others?

I was charged to write a paper setting forth the views of the founders. Issued in 1944, this was our Declaration of Independence, and I was the closest approach to its Thomas Jefferson. However, wanting Jefferson's genius, I had to labor through forty-four drafts. Comments on the early drafts often filled a folder as thick as a Methodist hymn book. For every five words I wrote, I crossed out seven. The resulting document, entitled *The Economics of a Free Society* and originally published in *Fortune*,[23] has been flatteringly described as cur "articles of faith."[24] It began with twelve dedicatory points, the first of which reads:

> The good of all—the common good—is a means to the enduring happiness of every individual in society and is superior to the economic interest of any private group, not only in war (when the validity of the principle is obvious) but in peace as well.

Point 4 leads off with a concession to the much maligned Tennessee Valley Authority:

> In a democracy there is a place for private enterprise and there is a place for public enterprise, and it is necessary to clarify basic lines of division between them. The area for private enterprise should extend to the limit of the ability of private individuals better to serve the common good. Beyond this limit, government enterprise can better serve that good.

Point 8 confesses a belief in collective bargaining and intimates that Franklin D. Roosevelt was not wholly wrong:

> To compensate for the weakness of their individual bargaining position, wage earners need the right to combine into organizations for collective bargaining. Provided that the power of these organizations is not permitted to stifle technical progress, or unduly to limit access to jobs, or in other ways to be abused, labor unions can serve the common good.

Point 10 suggests there is something to be said for Lord Keynes after all:

> Prolonged and severe depressions, as the result of which millions lose their savings and their jobs, cannot be accepted as natural and irremediable phenomena. The people's elected representatives and the agencies of government are responsible for establishing fiscal, monetary, and other policies that help prevent the fever of inflation and the paralysis of deflation and depression. Constructive policies respecting taxation and public expenditures (including expenditures for public works), intelligent handling of the national debt, and enlightened control over credit and money can greatly retard or prevent excessive swings of the business cycle. Consistent governmental policies that conform to the community's standards of justice, and that are understood by the community, are vital both for developing consumer and business confidence and for maintaining the flow of buying power needed to sustain high levels of employment and productivity.

The paper closes by reaffirming the belief "that ignorance of economic processes must give way to understanding and intelligent action," and the last paragraph states:

> We in America have always had a dream. We have never lost it. We have it now. With the enterprise, initiative, and good will of man urged on to the common good, we can make that dream come alive—not in the millennium but in the America of the approaching tomorrow.

Why, I ask, should we want the aims of CED in the future to be other than those of the past? Can we not still agree that the enterprise system must work not merely for those with enterprise, but, more importantly, for the common good of all? Let us then try to do better and better what we set out to do, and what we have been attempting to do, these twenty-five years. Let us continue to provide a source of leadership for the business community in order to guide the country toward a new frontier. And, may I add, toward a great society.

I do not put these phrases "new frontier" and "great society" in capital letters. I gladly concede to my Republican friends their right and duty to improve on such hopeful political slogans. However, I do not believe that any of us, or any other organization, is likely to improve on the aims to which we were originally dedicated and to which we can rededicate ourselves—with candor, without reservations, and, I hope, with 1942's enthusiasm.

Business Was the Whipping Boy of the Depression

CLARENCE FRANCIS

Though my primary purpose is to look to the future, it may be useful first to recall the conditions at the time CED was founded. Remember that all through the 1930's, business was the whipping boy of the Great Depression. Government was transcendent while business was blamed for the nation's ills—unemployment, poverty, and everything but dust storms and crop failures. Moreover, the doctrine of "economic maturity" was being proclaimed. We were being told that we had about reached the limit of our economic growth with few new frontiers to explore.

Then came World War II and the absolute necessity for government-business cooperation in industrial mobilization with nothing less than national survival at stake. All feuds forgotten, we closed ranks in the war effort. We learned a great deal from that experience, and from it we developed a new sense of the possibilities of the future. But remember also that it was then widely assumed that the war's end would bring another depression with an estimated 8 million unemployed.

This, then, was the atmosphere in which CED came into being. A few businessmen met to discuss the role that business leadership could play in minimizing unemployment and in shaping a future of postwar growth and prosperity—*not* just for themselves, *not* just for their companies, but for the progress and self-betterment of all our people. From this point on, business began to speak with a new voice. Indeed, it spoke a new language: the language of corporate responsibility to the public, of business-government cooperation on matters of economic and social development, and of national decisions based on solid research and calm discussion. It was, in short, the language of vision, of courage, and of confidence in the future.

A real turning point in approach and attitude came when CED organized a frontal attack to prevent postwar unemployment across the nation. Local committees everywhere instilled spirit and hope and gave valuable aid to businesses, small and large. Communities responded with new ideas, new products, new equipment, and new jobs. The predictions of widespread unemployment proved false. The nation was put on the road to an era of growth and progress that has continued to this day.

For the past quarter of a century, the CED's recommendations, arising from its research and discussions, often have pointed out the right turn in the road or opened up new views of the possibilities of the future. These have led to policies of sound business-government cooperation on matters affecting the public interest. And always these have been based on the precious principle of free enterprise—the dynamic mainspring of our national growth, progress, and strength, and the true source of freedom itself.

During these past years, we have witnessed many wonders. There have been explosive developments in mechanization, automation, transportation, communication, and the growth of the population, and the end is not in sight. We are facing new wonders in electronics, in atomic energy, in the ocean, and in space. The underlying great wonder is the system of business enterprise which has given such great impetus to all our gains. Government and industry are learning the wisdom of cooperative action.

For the future, then, what is the role of CED? One of the greatest challenges of our time, I believe, lies in the problems—economic, social, and environmental—of our cities. The trend of population has been away from the farms into the cities. The age of urbanization is upon us and there is no turning back. Urban affairs thus become a definite operating responsibility of business management. Our researches can help point the way to the city of the future—prosperous, harmonious, and clean—where people really can enjoy living and working. Jobs and housing are still the basic needs of many people.

Other great challenges lie in oceanography, in supersonic transportation, in space, and all the other areas of opportunity that confront us today. Imagination and foresight are needed. We must find the means of developing quickly and abundantly the new wonders that can minimize poverty, pain, and war. And the greatest challenge of all is for government and industry to preserve the principle of business enterprise and freedom of economic choice—of the sanctity of work versus security.

The future belongs to a new generation of leadership, to men who accept the responsibility of operating business profitably in the interest of the entire community and of energizing economic development in every area. The goal today, as it was twenty-five years ago, is jobs and opportunity—not dependency and degradation—for all citizens. Now, as then, the answer to the challenges of the future will depend on the wisdom and vision of decisions yet to be made; these will depend in turn on the quality and soundness of the information on which they are based.

We Dared Not Leave Economic Solutions to Chance

THOMAS B. McCABE

There is some virtue in celebrating anniversaries because it gives an organization the opportunity to determine how far it has come from its initial founding to the present and to what extent its objectives and policies have changed in the interim. As a surveyor turns his telescope backward to obtain his benchmarks, it is fitting that we recheck the past in order to determine if our program has been sound and if the effort and money have been expended profitably. But in looking back, we must not become so proud of our past that complacency develops and we lose sight of the challenge of the present and future.

As Clarence Francis points out, CED was organized in 1942 by a group of business leaders who were convinced that the solution of postwar economic problems could not be left to chance. We were still close to the days of the early 1930's. We knew that we dared not face another period of such unemployment. And we knew that if we did, the chances for our way of life were dim. We determined to put everything we had into an effort to avoid that calamity. We knew that government would have to play its part, probably the major part.

Accomplishment of our original goal required: first, the development of positive programs for resolving problems; second, a program to educate leaders of commerce and industry at the grass roots throughout the country; third, an effective and objective presentation of its views to the policy-making officials of government. Through its continuous research program, CED has made constructive contributions to the solutions of many types of economic problems.

A searching analysis of CED's past is reassuring in spite of the fact that it has had its ups and downs. Fortunately, there was only one period of a year or two when we were seriously concerned about its effectiveness, and then we went rapidly into action. As a result of thorough study, we determined that the objectives were sound and the policies were excellent; the primary weakness was found to lie in administration and selection procedures in connection with the trustees. As soon as these deficiencies were corrected, we began to go forward.

If what CED has to say on public questions commands wide attention and respect, this is because it has never spoken from the standpoint of narrow interest. The cross-fertilization of ideas between leaders in industry and the professions has given CED its status in the eyes of the academic world as a responsible spokesman from the world of commerce and industry on economic and social problems. It likewise explains why more and more public officials turn to CED for counsel and assistance, as I did when I was Chairman of the Board of Governors of the Federal Reserve System. I found CED gave me more aid in its statements on monetary and credit problems than any other group of business or financial people, especially in the very critical period prior to the Treasury-Federal Reserve accord, which was reached in 1951.

With such a reputation goes a heavy responsibility—especially in this time of trial and test of American institutions.

What's Good for the World Is Good for the U.S.A.

PAUL G. HOFFMAN

Back in the late 1930's there was a poster that dramatized the thinking then prevalent in a large sector of American business. A stern, finger-pointing executive admonished viewers to believe that "What's good for business is good for you." The founding fathers of CED, however, were of another opinion and altered the wording to "What's good for the U.S.A. is good for business." The slogan has gone through still another metamorphosis, for it is my conviction that the enlightened business community now readily accepts the view that "What's good for the *world* is good for the U.S.A."

There is a growing realization that the problems of our country and those of our world are so closely interrelated that most of them can only be solved if we accept and act on the idea that our world in many vital respects is one indivisible community. This does not mean the setting up of a world government. It does mean the creation of a world in which there is growing respect for a body of international law and the greatest possible degree of international cooperation. For if nations are willing to surrender some measure of their traditional sovereignty, to accept and capitalize on their diversity, to live as tolerant good neighbors, to work together for a rapidly expanding world economy, our dream of a better world can be realized. But if nations and individuals are not willing to move in this direction, then it is our nightmares that are likely to become a reality.

The kind of world I envision will not be achieved in our generation and perhaps not even in the next. But progress *can* be made now. And in the achievement of that progress, business has a trailblazing role to play. I see this leadership responsibility falling into five specific areas.

First of all, enlightened business leadership must continue to provide sound guidance in domestic affairs, for just as the course of world events deeply affects America, so what happens here in the United States has a major impact on the rest of the world. Moreover, of all the great countries in the world the United States has, the best opportunity, I believe, to become a truly great society. What do I mean when I speak of "a great society"? Many years ago Beardsley Ruml suggested to me that the goal for which the whole world should strive was the creation of societies in which every child would have the opportunity to realize fully his potentials for growth—material, intellectual, and spiritual. I was deeply struck by this idea when he first expressed it. Today I feel even more strongly that this course is the only right one for the United States—right both in terms of morality and in terms of common sense.

Second, the business community must continue to promote international thinking. This is a natural role for it, because much of business today is becoming international, and international business by its very nature thinks beyond national borders. International business wants a world in which it can trade freely—trade not only goods and services, but ideas and techniques as well. And one of the most profitable results of such trade is the development of friendly economic contacts that can pave the way for closer and more friendly political relationships.

Third, business leaders must continue to bring their influence to bear on behalf of economic integration in the developing regions of Asia, Africa, and Latin America where international business is active. This is essential both to the promotion of prosperity and the strengthening of peace. To illustrate just how much economic integration can help in advancing both these goals, one has only to look back on the results of the Marshall Plan. From the earliest days of that program, we who were involved in its activities had very much in mind the eventual creation of a common market for all of Europe. Thanks to the work of Jean Monnet, Paul-Henri Spaak, and others, great progress has been made toward that end; and someday it will be completely achieved. Already the economic integration of the Inner Six has not only done much to assure their economic well-being; it has also created a situation that makes the outbreak of a new European war well-nigh impossible and that perforce has moved the continent toward closer political union.

Next, business must work to foster investments and other economic activities by private enterprise in the world's developing countries. The participation of private enterprise in the low-income countries' development is already sizable. But even from a purely economic standpoint, that participation is by no means as great as it should be, considering the fact that the 1.5 billion people who live in the low-income countries constitute a great new economic frontier. Already these people are good customers, buying goods and services from the industrialized nations at the rate of some $25 billion a year. And with even modest increases in their per capita incomes, that figure could be doubled or tripled within the foreseeable future.

Let me add that efforts required to realize this vast economic promise would cost the industrialized nations relatively little. At present the flow of development assistance from the richer to the poorer countries is about $7.5 billion a year net. Most authorities agree that this figure should be increased to a net of $15 billion by 1970, an estimate based on the best available calculations both of the needs of developing countries and of their capacity usefully to absorb external aid. Taken by itself, this projected $15 billion of external assistance represents a sizable sum. But its apparent magnitude dwindles greatly when one compares it with the gross national product of the richer countries, which is even now estimated at nearly $1.5 trillion and is steadily growing. To put it another way, we are talking about an expenditure for development assistance totaling perhaps 1 per cent of the industrialized countries' GNP, and as any businessman knows, a 1 per cent investment in market expansion is a very modest investment indeed.

Finally, I believe that the business community must lend maximum possible support to today's global war against both material poverty and poverty of opportunity. In fact, I think this is the most important contribution that governments, businesses, or private individuals can make toward building a more peaceful world, inasmuch as there is an intimate relationship between poverty and threats to the peace. As Robert S. McNamara pointed out in a speech to the American Association of Newspaper Editors, nearly 90 per cent of all those many countries where per capita incomes are $100 a year or less suffered an average of two major and violent internal upheavals between 1958 and 1967. Moreover, since the end of World War II, every single outbreak of armed hostilities between nations has had its roots in the less-developed parts of the world where great masses of people suffer from hunger, ignorance, disease, destitution, and poverty of opportunity. Let me stress again the phrase "poverty of opportunity." For it is not poverty alone but the lack of opportunities for betterment that lies at the root of the unrest and open violence that troubles so much of the world, including our own United States.

Here, then, are some of the major tasks—and they are enormous ones—confronting CED. I wish I could prophesy that the first twenty-five years of CED would turn out to have been its hardest. But I think that would be unrealistic. For the world as a whole may well be facing in the remaining years of this century the most difficult problems and tasks that have ever confronted civilized mankind.

We Have Yet to Achieve National Economic Literacy

W. WALTER WILLIAMS

Sometimes a glimpse into the past helps in setting goals for the future. After a frustrating telephone conversation in his office at SHAEF, General Eisenhower once remarked that sometimes one had to look back to see whence he had come and the obstacles that had been surmounted to gain determination and vision to face the future. So a little glimpse of CED's past may be both informative and stimulating.

In May, 1948, Harry Johnston, CED's Executive Director, requested me to accompany him to the University Club in New

York to attend an important committee meeting. Its purpose was to come up with recommendations to the Board of Trustees as to what CED's future should be. The meeting was about to adjourn on a negative note. After all, the war was over; the Field Division, which had mobilized some 70,000 business leaders in 3,000 American communities, had been disbanded; Paul Hoffman had resigned to head up the Marshall Plan; the 90 per cent excess profits tax had been repealed; and no one could be found to take on the chairmanship to succeed Paul Hoffman. All in all, the spirit of "let's go home and call it a day" prevailed.

Although not a member of the committee, I offered the thought that if the economic research process of CED had been worth while in considering the problems of transition from a wartime economy to a peacetime economy, surely there must be justification for the continuation of CED's research mechanism—Paul Hoffman has described it as "a collaboration between the campus and the counting house"—in dealing with the economic problems of the postwar period. The meeting adjourned.

A few days later the semiannual meeting of CED was held. My name begins with "W" and "W" is very close to the bottom of the alphabet. There is a very close relationship between this simple fact and the equally simple fact that the board, reaching into the very bottom of the barrel in sheer desperation, was obliged to tag me with the chairmanship to succeed Paul Hoffman.

We had many problems. Financing was one, for money was no longer easy to come by with the 90 per cent excess profits tax out the window. Leadership by the Chairman of the Research and Policy Committee was vital if the research activities were to continue. Thanks to such stalwarts as Donald K. David and Charles E. Wilson of General Electric Company, Philip D. Reed was prevailed upon to take on this important assignment.

This brief review of CED at a critical turning point in its history does indeed give us determination and vision to tackle the future. For there is yet *so* much to do. Consider, for instance, the field of economic education. In 1949, CED held an all-day conference on economic education. John Studebaker, then United States Commissioner of Education, made this significant statement: "[Only] about 7 per cent of our high school students get any kind of an economic education at all, and that is of very poor quality." Later, speaking to the New England Council in Boston, I quoted Studebaker. The next day there came a telephone call from the Federal Reserve Bank of Boston. Had I made the 7 per cent statement? Yes. Back came the response, "You're wrong, it's only 5.6 per cent. I obtained this figure from the Department of Health, Education, and Welfare just today."

Whether 5.6 per cent or 7 per cent, the figure is appallingly low. When we consider the close relationship between the quality of our economic understanding and the quality of political institutions, these percentages become even more appalling. The more so for CED, in view of our basic tenet, cited by William Benton, that "ignorance of economic processes must give way to understanding and intelligent action." Though CED has devoted twenty-five years of effort to this cause, we have barely started toward contributing our share in the building of a better America through the development of a nation of economic and political literates. Let us be cheered by our past accomplishments, but let us regard them merely as stepping stones for greater achievements in the future.

National Aims Require Stable Economic Growth

FRAZAR B. WILDE

CED has always warned against the risks of prophecy. Nevertheless, it is vital for an on-going institution to look not only at its current outlook but also at its longer future. The basic question is simple: Will there be any need for CED during the next quarter of a century? That will depend upon the competency of CED to make useful contributions to whatever may be the important national problems. That there will be national problems of magnitude no one of us can doubt.

The major categories of present and future problems are in three sectors: (1) the domestic and worldwide threat of overpopulation; (2) the threats around the world to peace and stability; and (3) economic problems, domestic and international.

On several occasions, CED has advocated voluntary family planning as a means of curbing the growing menace of overpopulation, particularly throughout the low-income countries of the world. Though I am sure we shall continue to urge appropriate means to this end, I believe that other groups and organizations are better suited than CED to carry on effective work in the field of population control. Nor do we visualize a job for us in the area of peace and war, except in the terms of international cooperation and trade that Paul Hoffman mentions.

The third category, embracing economic problems, has many facets, several of which have been of deep concern to this group over the years and most certainly will continue to be matters of continuing interest and study. The first of these subcategories is the field of fiscal and monetary policy, which has been CED's central concern throughout its history. A second area of deep interest is education, with emphasis on how it can be properly extended to cope with new social problems and the challenge of new methods. Next comes the better management of federal, state, and local institutions, taking into account the specific problems involved in programs for the rehabilitation of metropolitan areas and in the proper division of responsibility as among federal, state, and local bodies in terms both of money and management. Finally, there is the task of seeking a balance between our international objectives and our means of accomplishing these ends—a task made easier by partnership than by going it alone.

As in the past, CED's major contribution is likely to be in the fiscal and monetary field. After all, success in this area is vital to all our problems. Ever since the Employment Act of 1946, the nation has been challenged to implement the act. CED has directed great effort to this end through the development of budgetary, fiscal, and monetary programs calculated to promote steady growth, high employment, and stable prices. Not only is this kind of domestic progress vital in achieving the national purpose, but it is equally important because of the United States' world responsibilities.

Our record in the past gives some hope for believing that we can produce more goods and services for more people—and it is essential that this be done—through non-inflationary, stable growth. However, the recent record, from the fall of 1965 on, obviously has been on the sad side. To get back on the track and stay on the track is going to take continuous, steady, and aggressive action from those relatively few who understand the score. Let us continue to devote our energies to this complicated field, where we can make our most valuable contribution.

We Must Seek the Who, Where, Why of Poverty

RALPH E. FLANDERS

There is a popular misunderstanding of the published figures on unemployment. When the Bureau of Labor Statistics announces that in the month of July, 1967, for instance, the figure was 3.9 per cent of the labor force, most of us assume that only 3.9 per cent of those able to work or wanting work or who ought to work are unemployed. This conclusion is false. The "labor force" is by no means the whole body of the population who can work and ought to work. This fact is responsible for an unjustified and dangerous complacency. In any event, 3.9 per cent is higher than warranted by "frictional unemployment."

When I was a member of the Joint Economic Committee during my years as Senator, from 1946 to 1958, the testimony in the course of our poverty study tended to discount city poverty as against rural poverty. In the cities, most of the poor were in the labor force, hence they suffered only periodic unemployment and had the backstop of unemployment compensation. Now conditions have changed. By hook or by crook, hundreds of thousands of the unemployed rural poor have managed to migrate to the cities, and we can no longer be complacent about urban poverty with these new and hopeless additions.

Rural poverty has now come to public attention. Following a Senatorial tour of the Mississippi Delta, a team of physicians visited the area and examined many hundreds of children.[25] Great numbers of them were suffering from malnutrition so serious that it verged on starvation. The photographs reproduced in this article gave the clue to the causes of poverty in this particular region. In the same room with food on the table that obviously had little nutritional value were an electrical or gas refrigerator and a bottled-gas stove. This family is only one of the many families in the Delta who are victims of the mechanization of cotton growing and picking. They constitute a special though serious case.

There is long-standing poverty as well. Anyone who has traveled the South by car or train must have seen evidence of chronic poverty in the pine barrens and elsewhere. It affects poor whites as well as poor Negroes, the Appalachian region being a case in point.

It has seemed to me for some time that we must find out the who, where, and why of both rural and urban poverty. One immediately thinks of the 1970 census as a means of answering these questions. Objection is reasonably made that this complicates the enumeration beyond the abilities of the ordinary enumerator. But how else shall we get at the problem? The only endeavor to analyze total unemployment that I have seen is a review of then current research by Dwight Macdonald in the *New Yorker*, back in January, 1963, under the title "Our Invisible Poor." Much has happened since then.

When we get the true dimensions of unemployment, it may well be that our country will find itself among the backward nations in this respect, certainly ranking below Europe. In my judgment this is the most serious domestic problem our country faces. I see no solution in the proposed negative income tax; to finance a permanent caste of paupers is un-American. The problem needs the devoted consideration of the best brains in the United States. In its own long-range interest and for the public good, American business should take the lead.

Millions of Workers Still Lack Adequate Benefits

MARION B. FOLSOM

My remarks are concerned broadly with the role and responsibility of businessmen and business organizations in social progress. But first I would like to discuss briefly the activities of the Business Advisory Council (BAC),* which led up to the organization of CED.

As early as November, 1940, the BAC's Economic Policy Committee, of which I was then chairman, was asked to study the role of the BAC during the war and postwar periods. In June, 1941, our committee reported that it was quite important that we do not look entirely to the federal government for a solution of postwar problems, but that everything should be done to encourage private enterprise to assist in getting ready for the new era. In November, 1941, we recommended that the U.S. Department of Commerce and the BAC take a prominent part

*The present name, the Business Council, was adopted in 1961.

in the formation of a new organization for postwar planning. With the help of the Under Secretary of Commerce, Wayne Chatfield Taylor, we began discussions with business and government economists and circulated a questionnaire to business concerns to see what planning they were doing. In March, 1942, we submitted our recommendation for the formation of a postwar planning organization to be undertaken jointly by private enterprise and the Department of Commerce listing six definite functions.

At a meeting on April 9, 1942, the chairman of the Council was authorized to appoint a committee of five to work with Secretary of Commerce Jesse H. Jones and Taylor, both of whom were very much interested. Secretary Jones felt that the membership should not be confined to the members of the Council, and with his wide acquaintance among business people, he brought together a group of eighteen from various sections of the country, who became the first eighteen trustees of CED. At this meeting, while Paul Hoffman was out taking a telephone call, the group decided that he was the logical man to serve as chairman of the new organization.

For some time before this, both Paul Hoffman and William Benton had been working on a plan to bring together a group of business people, economists, and social scientists to discuss broad national economic policy issues. At Hoffman's suggestion, Benton and I discussed a merger of the two programs, and prior to the organization meeting, several of us had agreed on the two objectives: First, to stimulate and assist businessmen to prepare for a high level of employment after the war; second, to conduct objective research and issue statements on general economic policy for the country as a whole. Hoffman suggested that Ralph Flanders be made Chairman of the Research Committee and asked me to be Chairman of the Field Development Division. You all know the story from that time on.

A most significant measure of social progress in a nation is the protection provided the worker and his dependents against the economic hazards of life—accidents, ill health, dependent old age, unemployment, premature death. This protection can be provided by the individual, the employer, or the government, or any combination of the three. Prior to the 1930's, this country depended largely upon the individual to provide this protection. In 1935, the unemployment and old-age insurance plans were adopted to serve as the basic protection to prevent workers from being dependent upon relief.

Since then, particularly after World War II, there has been a tremendous development of voluntary benefit plans by employers providing supplemental pensions, sickness benefits, group life insurance, and health insurance. The cost of these plans now amounts to about 25 per cent of payroll, with cost as high as 40 or 45 per cent in some cases. The employees of practically all large companies and well-established companies of all sizes now have good protection against these major hazards from the government plans, the employee benefit and thrift plans, and from their own savings.

This marked increase in fringe benefits, along with the steady rise in real wages, has brought about a substantial increase in our standard of living. Of course, the prime responsibility of business management is to continue to devote its efforts to improve productivity, which is the basis of our progress. However, the manager—as an individual member of society and as an employer—is now becoming more concerned about the conditions of those in the lowest-income groups, who, while better off than similar groups a generation ago, have not participated greatly in these increased benefits and protection.

There are still many millions of workers who do not have this protection, and these same workers generally receive lower wages. It should be noted that pressure from the low-income groups has led in the past to compulsory governmental plans.

Estimates indicate that about 30 per cent of employees in industry—except in four states with compulsory legislation—do not receive sickness benefits for absence because of illness; about 20 per cent do not have the protection of group life insurance or health insurance plans; and about 40 per cent are not employed in companies with supplemental pension plans. These are the employees of smaller concerns, especially in service trades, and casual workers, and their principal protection comes from the governmental old-age and unemployment insurance plans, and workmen's compensation. In case of serious illness, long periods of unemployment, early death of the wage earner, these families are apt to become dependent on relief.

The record of organized business in relation to governmental plans designed primarily to help the lower-income groups has not been a very good one. Probably the most significant development in recent years has been the growth of the federal old-age insurance plan, adopted in 1935, which has now reached the point where 24 million persons—aged, survivors, and dependents—are receiving monthly benefit checks as a matter of right because of prior contributions. Many of these would otherwise be dependent upon relief. Yet, during the early stages, organized business had very little to do with the development of this far-reaching system, leaving it up to a few individuals to present a business point of view and assist in putting it on a sound basis.

For instance, the Chamber of Commerce of the United States did not favor the principles of Social Security until 1942, when a referendum of the local chambers resulted in a two-thirds favorable vote. The National Association of Manufacturers did not reverse its attitude of opposition until 1950, when labor controversies regarding supplementary pension plans brought home to the leaders the value of the basic federal plan.

The only business organization that supported Social Security in the early years was the Business Advisory Council. There were four of us on the BAC who had served on the advisory committee which helped to draft the legislation. We kept the BAC members well informed, and they understood the problems and proposals. The trouble with the other organizations was mainly a lack of objective approach and understanding by the leaders, as well as inept staff work.

That we are still faced with this lack of objective approach and understanding was indicated by the opposition of organized business and particularly of organized medicine to Medicare. If it had not been for this strong opposition, we probably would have gotten the moderate program recommended by the representative advisory committee and by the Administration, with the government plan being confined to hospital insurance for the aged and with all other medical costs being left to private agencies. This would also have avoided the large government subsidy of Part B (medical services).

It is my opinion that the greatest contribution of CED has been the demonstration to the business world of the value of thorough study, with the aid of competent academic advisors. From this can be derived an objective approach and the courage to issue statements of conclusions and recommendations, based on the considered judgment of the committee members. As an illustration, CED is still the only national business organization that has favored federal aid to education. We have recommended that aid be given public schools in the states that have per capita income considerably below the average of all states, and we have likewise urged increased expenditures at all levels of government to improve the education of disadvantaged children in the poverty areas.[26]

We are all concerned now about the conditions of the inner cities. I would suggest that employers have their economists and industrial relations people obtain facts about health, education, and housing conditions in their cities. Unless your city is an exception, it will be found that the nonwhite children reach first grade one year behind typical white youngsters and that they are two years behind at the sixth grade and three years by high school; that the elementary schools do not participate in the hot lunch programs although all suburban schools do; that about four times as many homes are dilapidated; that the tuberculosis rate in this area is probably ten times that of the outer city of suburbs and the infant mortality is two and a half times greater.

I would also suggest that the industrial relations people, who are naturally concerned with all the benefits and welfare of their fellow employees, devote some of their time and talents to the work of the voluntary agencies in these poverty areas; and especially to see that they adjust their programs to meet these current conditions.

We Travel to the Stars but Live in Slums

DONALD K. DAVID

Together we created a new way for private citizens to work on public problems. Together we shaped policies that have helped the American economy achieve an unprecedented record of sustained growth. Together we promoted economic progress abroad as well as at home. We have shared many battles, a few defeats, and some notable victories. But the past always has been but the starting blocks for the race to new goals, which is the best use of the past.

Before CED, business was looked upon generally as the entrenched defender of an unsatisfactory status quo. Then came World War II, followed by the necessity of shifting the economy from total war to partial peace and adjusting to a new position of responsibility in the world. CED was born of the necessity for business to be a leader in planning and achieving a rapid change from war to peace wth a minimum of dislocation.

Now we face the same challenge. What will peace bring to our economy? And what is CED doing to anticipate it? To these questions we must respond. There are those who question what we are doing today. That is good. The number and variety of problems to choose from should make the setting of priorities a matter of constant contention. But there should be no question whatever about the validity of the mission itself.

While we accept change as a fact of life, it is the accelerating pace of change that we are not yet used to. More change has occurred in the last decade than in the previous century. As recently as 1960, for example, no less an authority than the Royal Astronomer of Britain was describing the idea of space travel as "bilge."

We are, indeed, traveling to the stars while still dwelling in the slums. Computers click out in seconds the answers to mathematical problems that only a few years ago would have taken decades to solve. This now occurs routinely in a world in which hundreds of millions of people—closer to us in time than Chicago was when CED was born—cannot yet write 2 and 2 equals 4 on a piece of paper. Men in satellites look down on men squatting beside grass huts lighting their fires by rubbing two sticks together. And their leaders in many cases, soon will have the all-consuming fire of atomic weapons in their hands.

There are many such contrasts that dramatize the dilemmas of our times and warn us that much is out of joint. Fearful wars in our neighborhoods, an unpopular war halfway around the world, crime, a vicious cycle of life on welfare for millions, delinquency, racial tensions, dreadful urban congestion, violence to humanity and to nature—these and other issues that disturb us deeply all have their roots in the unprecedented rate of change that man has unleashed. None of us can say that business leadership is doing enough to meet these problems.

Should such a view of the times lead to despair? Definitely not. We can and must use the revolutions of knowledge and of technology that surround us to find effective solutions that are consistent with our private economic system. Never has it been more important for businessmen to be among the leaders in confronting the challenges of our era. The future of the private sector will be determined by the quality of that leadership.

Having spent my life in both business and education, I am especially aware of the staggering needs of our privately supported colleges and universities as they try to face responsibly the demands our changing world is thrusting upon them. Their position is critical.

Business must do more to support them. Instead of a fraction of 1 per cent of profits which they are now providing, business must increase its contributions closer to the 5 per cent the tax laws allow. Business needs to invest more in the intellectual resources that our educational institutions can provide. And the world needs the guidance and wisdom that the best of business and the best of the academic community, working together, can provide.

It is the inventive and vigorous brain of man that has created most of the problems that plague us. Out of the same brain can be summoned the new attitudes, new policies, new institutions, and adaptations of old ones that such creativity requires.

What Will a Trillion Dollar Utopia Be Like?

HARRY SCHERMAN

The future aims of any group such as CED must take into account the nation's certain continued economic growth. If the past long-term growth averages persist, it is not unlikely that within a few years our gross national product will pass the trillion mark measured by constant dollars—and who knows what in inflationary dollars. What problems, in terms of changed economic relationships and in general living conditions, will such a GNP bring?

As the subtitle implies, CED's 1958 policy statement on *Economic Growth in the United States: Its Past and Future* did consider to some extent future economic growth. However, as I look back upon that study, the notions it presented were highly generalized. Actually, no organized inquiry into the future was conducted by the committee at the time. What I visualize now is a really thorough study, spanning several years, if need be, and possibly carried on in cooperation with other bodies.

Some of the principal areas of certain change that would have to be covered by such a study are evident enough even now. The most interesting to my own mind would be the spreading influences of a further increase in leisure time. As weekly working hours go down from 40 to 35 to 30 and perhaps lower, and as higher incomes result in generally earlier retirement, what effects can be foreseen on travel, on sports, on the various forms of communication, on reading, on the performing arts—not to speak of the purely economic effects on the immense variety of manufactured products having close association with leisure?

Another certain area of big change will be the further expansion of service activities of all kinds, which has been so noticeable in the total economic picture in recent years. This is bound to be still further magnified and will be particularly true of governmental services, which will burgeon further in both old and new directions and will surely bring new political differences, new problems of public decision. Also it should even now be possible to foresee quite a few new technological changes that may have vital, even revolutionary, influence on the way we all live, such as the utilization of ocean depths for foods and minerals. Another area certain to be basically influenced by far more leisure and far more income is education.

These few suggestions are presented only as examples of the future trends we can reasonably expect from our certain continued economic growth, which within a short period will result in a situation fairly describable as a material utopia. However, as an old man looking back on quite a long period of growth, I should not be surprised if that income-utopia presents us with even more worries than those we now have. That is why I think it would be wise to do some real research to prepare for them.

9. Needed: More "Dangerous" Men

CLARENCE C. WALTON

In view of the awesome quality of today's questions it is easy to conclude that never before have so few leaders been confronted with so many of what Bismarck once called "the imponderables." Nevertheless, overriding concerns with our immediate issues can blind leadership to the fact that every generation had to cope with its own special problems—problems that, because they have now been solved, seem miniscule when compared to contemporary complications.

It is an appeal for perspective, not simply for nostalgia's sake, that leads Clarence Francis to recall the problems faced by business a quarter of a century ago. "Remember," says Francis, "that all through the 1930's, business was the whipping boy of the Great Depression. Government was transcendent while business was blamed for the nation's ills—unemployment, poverty, and everything but dust storms and crop failures." But then came World War II, with its necessity for government and business cooperation. "We learned a great deal from that experience," remarks Francis, "and from it we developed a new sense of the possibilities of the future."

Historian William E. Leuchtenburg has described the early 1930 period as one when "like cold bay fog, fear of the bread line drifted up into the middle class." It is worth pausing for a moment to recall a few of the dreadful circumstances that engendered this fear:

> Thousands of university graduates took a diploma with no prospect of employment; marriages were postponed and the birth rate slipped from 18.8 to 17.4 per thousand; construction was halted; freight shipments were cut in half between 1929 and 1932; major railroad systems like the Chicago and Northwestern, the Wabash and the Missouri Pacific passed into receivership.[27]

It was, in short, a period when American business was put to trial by ordeal.

The Intellectual Challenge

If the performance during the 1930's justified a "guilty" verdict, to many the wartime achievements provided ample grounds for vindication.[28] However, the opportunity to renew confidence in the enterprise system could easily have been muffed, because—as Thomas B. McCabe rightly observes—many segments in the private sector remained committed to the principle of automaticity in economic affairs. Since business cycles were presumed to be as inevitable as life and death, government intervention in business was therefore anathema. Influental organizations such as the Chamber of Commerce of the United States and the National Association of Manufacturers espoused the very principles that Messrs. Benton, Ruml, Folsom *et al.* were preparing to challenge.

In McCabe's reflection of those days a quarter of a century ago, business leadership was still committed to dogmas more appropriate to an eighteenth-century world of petty shopkeepers than to a twentieth-century society dependent in heavy measure on the corporate giants. This view is also underscored by Paul Hoffman's observation that the thinking of one element of the business community was dramatized by a poster on which "a stern, finger-pointing executive admonished viewers to believe that 'What's good for business is good for you.' " By contrast, says Hoffman, the founding fathers of CED "were of another opinion and altered the wording to 'What's good for the U.S.A. is good for business.' "

The whole McCabe-Hoffman assessment is critical. At the very least, it is by implication a subtle yet significant modification of certain fundamental philosophical principles of western democracy and of western business respectively. Specifically, the challenge is directed against John Locke and Adam Smith, who provided the apologetic for the sanctity of property rights and for laissez-faire economics, respectively. Both had argued that the enlightened pursuit of private utilities *automatically* assured the achievement of public utilities; the public interest was the sum of private interests. In short, a businessman who kept his shop in prosperous estate kept the ship of state afloat.

If, however, the common good was something *more* than the sum of the individual parts, a very critical and practical question arose: How is this *bono publico* to be achieved? Again McCabe provides reinforcing testimony in observing that the country simply could not rest secure in accepting the beneficences of the automatically run market system as the surest guarantor of full employment and prosperity. In effect, the question being asked was: If the market system was a human creation, could it not be improved by human planning? His colleagues reiterate the point that while the stimulation of postwar planning was a vital and immediate goal, business could meet its full responsibility to American life only through continuing research that would identify those economic policies that had to be followed if the potentials of our free enterprise system were to be realized.

Clearly then, the enlightened sector of the business community, as represented by these men, was convinced that business had the primary responsibility for staving off a postwar economic disaster by providing high employment. Further, this could only come about if all business, both big and small, cooperated in the planning. Furthermore, research into economic policy was the *sine qua non* if leadership was to provide solutions designed to sustain economic stability and continued growth.[29]

The nature of the challenge has been cryptically described in these words: "The new approach differs from the older orthodoxy in reflecting the influence of Keynesian economics as well as of classical economics. As yet it is restricted to the CED and a few other managerial sources, such as *Fortune,* and receives comparatively little general repetition in the creed."[30] The critique, pronounced roughly a decade ago, would have to be substantially modified today because many economists, public-policy formulators, and corporate executives have adopted positions more congenial to the CED patterns; and these modifications in turn provide a fairly reliable index into the influence of an organization that, founded in 1942, sincerely expected to go out of business when peace returned. Indeed, as W. Walter Williams recalls, it very nearly happened that "the spirit of 'let's go home and call it a day' prevailed."

At this point, Williams suggested that if objective and rigorous research functions had been worth while "in considering the problems of transition from a wartime economy to a peacetime economy, surely there must be some justification for the continuation of CED's research mechanism . . . in dealing with the economic problems of the postwar period." That conviction led to a strengthening of the Research and Policy Committee; men such as Donald K. David and Philip D. Reed were prevailed upon to take an important part in the committee's work. The undertaking was never easy, and Karl Schriftgiesser was able to say that "for CED merely to espouse a new policy—or even to apply an old policy to a new situation—for many years almost invariably won it rejection by the editors of *The Wall Street Journal.*"[31]

The Partial Record

Over the past twenty-five years or so, CED has been involved in many battles, either in a leading or supporting role, which is by no means to say that all these battles have been won. There have been defeats and only partial victories, as Donald David and his colleagues are all too aware. Much remains to be done to advance causes and principles that have yet to win full acceptance and to secure gains already achieved. Nonetheless, enough victories have been won in these years by the forces represented by these men to have changed the ambience, both national and international, in which business operates.

The high level of economic prosperity that the western nations, in particular the industrialized countries, have enjoyed almost continuously since the recovery from World War II is in very dramatic contrast to the appalling world depression of the 1930's. Business has been the engine of this prosperity, and it has flourished in large measure because the rules of the game have been judiciously changed so that there is greater equity at the same time that greater economic stability has been achieved through new national and international institutions and arrangements.

Taken by and large, the postwar innovations in national and international economic policy have worked with considerable success; indeed, in comparison with the record of past eras, their success might even be called phenomenal. Beginning with the Bretton Woods Conference at the end of World War II, the western nations laid the basis for a new international monetary system that has financed an unprecedented expansion of world trade and investment, facilitated by the successive lowerings of tariffs and barriers through the General Agreement on Tariffs and Trade. The men appearing in these pages played a role in these events. They were active in the passage of the Employment Act of 1946 which established the Council of Economic Advisers and the Joint Economic Committee of the Congress. This development opened a new era in domestic policy by committing the government to the goal of high employment and by providing tools and techniques for the rational management of the economy. Over the years, too, has come a growing acceptance of what CED has called "the stabilizing budget policy," which has brought about a greater understanding of how monetary, fiscal, and budgetary policy can be employed in dealing with fluctuations in the economy. To reflect on these achievements alone, among the many that have been made in social and economic policy, is to realize vividly the vast distance that business and government have traveled—together—over the past quarter of a century.

The Unfinished Business

Despite these advances, the elder generation of leaders finds no room for complacency. With quiet eloquence, Donald David reminds today's leadership that "we are, indeed, traveling to the stars while still dwelling in the slums." In addressing themselves to the future, the older men are acutely aware of the growing urgency of the problems confronting society and of the compelling need to take vigorous action. Examining the needs of the future in terms of that aspect of economic and social organization that has been his particular sphere of interest, each man sees the unfinished nature of the work that has thus far been accomplished. The mechanisms devised over the past few decades must be improved and expanded if they are to serve adequately the new needs and urgencies.

"Ever since the Employment Act of 1946, the nation has been challenged to implement the act," says Frazar Wilde, and in turn he challenges the business community to continue its work toward this end. Proper fiscal and monetary policies are requisite if society's many objectives are to be achieved, and it is to this end that CED has directed great effort. "Not only is this kind of domestic progress vital in achieving the national purpose," Wilde points out, "but it is equally important because of the United States' world responsibilities."

Substantial support for this latter theme comes from Paul Hoffman, who stresses the world outlook of today's enlightened business leaders as being essential to the future of the nation. According to Hoffman, "the problems of our country and those of our world are so closely interrelated that most of them can only be solved if we accept and act on the idea that our world is, in many vital respects, one indivisible community." He notes that this does not mean the setting up of a world government, but that "it does mean the creation of a world in which there is a growing respect for a body of international law and the greatest possible degree of international cooperation."

The necessary nexus between domestic and international affairs leads Hoffman to observe that the opportunity this country has to become a truly great society will set a goal and an ideal that every other country will seek to emulate. But business must continue to promote international thinking simply because business today is becoming international, and international business by its very nature thinks beyond national borders. This premise leads Hoffman logically to consider the importance of various programs for international economic cooperation; Hoffman summons businessmen "to bring their influence to bear on behalf of economic integration in the developing regions . . . where international business is active. This is essential both to the promotion of prosperity and the strengthening of peace."

Quite clearly because of his own role in directing the Marshall Plan and now as Administrator of the United Nations Development Program, Hoffman is driven to stress the importance of world community and of a paralleling economic integration. But since these goals for progress face a rough future, the business community must continue to encourage investments and other economic activities by private enterprise in the world's developing countries. These developing nations already buy goods and services from the industrial world at the rate of some $25 billion a year and modest increases in per capita incomes could double or triple this figure within the foreseeable future.

At the present time one cannot be unaware of the appalling differences between industrialized and developing nations. America grows in one year by more than the entire national income of India which has twice the American population; 75 per cent of the world's wealth is consumed by the Atlantic community which comprises 20 per cent of the world's population. Noting that the flow of assistance from richer to poorer countries only approximates $7.5 billion per year net (when experts agree that it should be double that figure by 1970), Hoffman argues that the apparent magnitude of the challenge "dwindles greatly when one compares it with the gross national product of the richer countries, which is even now estimated at nearly $1.5 trillion and is steadily growing." Put another way, says Hoffman, "we are talking about an expenditure for development assistance totaling perhaps 1 per cent of the industrialized countries' GNP, and as any businessman knows, a 1 per cent investment in market expansion is a very modest investment indeed."

Ralph Flanders turns his attention to another and equally appalling gap—that dividing the affluent Americans from the millions of their countrymen who live in poverty. Who are the poor? What really is poverty? These are the questions asked by Flanders.

The answers depend in some important respects on definition. In 1967 the poverty line was defined by the Social Security Administration as a four-person household money income falling below $3,335 a year (with adjustments for family size and the place of residence). But many observers feel that the definition is totally misleading and that poverty in America at the present time must be viewed basically as a matter of *economic and social distance*. On this basis, economist Victor R. Fuchs suggested we define the poor as "any family whose income is less than one half the median family income."[32] Certainly there is wisdom in this suggestion because it recognizes that minimum or subsistence budgets are based on contemporary standards that soon become obsolete; by defining poverty in a relationship context, therefore, a more accurate picture is given of the nation's groping toward policy with respect to distribution of income.

In the United States, the persistence of mass urban poverty is unique among the industrial democracies of the world. Daniel Moynihan has pointed out that "we are the only industrial democracy in the world that does not have a family allowance, and we are the only industrial democracy in the world whose streets are filled with rioters each summer."[33] One may challenge the Moynihan implication of a causal nexus between inadequate welfare programs and rioting, but one cannot ignore the grim reality of more than 26 million people living in poverty in a country producing a gross national output of more than $800 billion annually.

Flanders sees an overriding imperative to provide meaningful jobs as one major step toward alleviating the problem of poverty. Taking the Bureau of Labor Statistics report on the unemployment rate for July 1967 (3.9 per cent of the labor force), Flanders noted that it was generally concluded that less than 4 per cent of those able and willing to work—or who ought to work—were unemployed. But the figures are today misleading. Recalling his days of membership on the Joint Economic Committee of the Congress, Senator Flanders notes that testimony taken in the committee's poverty study discounted city poverty. "In the cities most of the poor were in the labor force, hence they suffered only periodic unemployment and had the backstop of unemployment compensation. Now conditions have changed. By hook or by crook hundreds of thousands of the unemployed rural poor have managed to migrate to the cities, and we can no longer be complacent about urban poverty with these new and hopeless additions." Persuaded that even now we have not perceived the true dimension of unemployment in our country, Flanders regards the necessity to provide satisfactory jobs as first among the national priorities. "In my judgment . . . [unemployment] is the most serious domestic problem our country faces."

While Senator Flanders stresses the importance of creating jobs for those outside the labor market, Marion Folsom focuses on those who are employed but who are not adequately protected against "the economic hazards of life"—sickness, accidents, old age, premature death of the bread winner, as well as unemployment. The needs of the lower-income groups are brought under special scrutiny by Folsom, who forthrightly says that the record of business "in relation to governmental plans designed primarily to help the lower-income groups has not been a very good one." He adds this warning: "[The] pressure from the low-income groups has led in the past to compulsory governmental plans."

Folsom marshalls dramatic figures in support of his thesis: Even today there are possibly 30 per cent of employees in industry (except in four states with compulsory legislation) who receive no sickness benefits for absenteeism caused by illness; another fifth of the working force have no protection through group life insurance or through health insurance plans; 40 per cent are not covered by supplemental pension plans. Finally, notes Folsom, this last and largest group "are the employees of smaller concerns, especially in service trades, and casual workers, and their principal protection comes from the governmental old-age and unemployment insurance plans, and workmen's compensation. In case of serious illness, long periods of unemployment, early death of wage earner, these families are apt to become dependent on relief."

Folsom, who was one of the authors of the Social Security system, has put his finger on a very significant area of unfinished business in American society. In effect, he is saying to the business community that once again, even after several decades of experience, it is avoiding its responsibility where a very serious social issue is involved. Further, he is asserting that business cannot have it both ways—that it cannot slough off the job itself and then hinder government from undertaking it.

The past record, Folsom notes, is not encouraging. "During the early stages, organized business had very little to do with the development of this far-reaching . . . [Social Security] system." He points out that the Chamber of Commerce of the United States did not favor the principles of Social Security until 1942, when a referendum of the local chambers resulted in a two-thirds favorable vote. Nor did the National Association of Manufacturers reverse its attitude of opposition until 1950, "when labor controversies regarding supplementary pension plans brought home to the leaders the value of the basic federal plan." Folsom adds that the only business organization that supported Social Security in the early years was the Business Advisory Council.

Because of his background in both business and education, it is to be expected that Donald David would address himself very directly to what he called "the staggering needs of our privately supported colleges and universities as they try to face responsibly the demands our changing world is thrusting upon them. Their position is critical."* He calls upon business to assume a greater responsibility for providing the funds that are so desperately needed for the continued existence of private higher education.

Historically the business community has not been indifferent to the financial needs of private colleges, but responsibilities toward education were discharged by businessmen from their own personal fortunes. As the editor observed on another occasion:

> It was perfectly permissible, for instance, for Arthur and Lewis Tappan (who attributed the success of their New York silk-importing business to the moral supervision of their clerks and to a strictly cash, one-price system of merchandising) to contribute to the founding of Oberlin and Kenyon; it was all right, too, when Abbott Lawrence and Samuel Appleton, New England industrialists, supported Amherst and Harvard with gifts from their own fortunes; it was even tolerable for James Smithson to leave approximately a half-million dollars to the American government to establish the Smithsonian Institution. But it is quite another matter for managers to give away that which they do not own; this substitution of group for individual conscience should be as distasteful to the current crop of executive managers as it was, say to William Ellery Channing back in

---

* The critical nature of the problem and its magnitude on a national scale can be judged by a recent study on private higher education in New York State. An expert examining committee came to the conclusion that "a combined annual deficit for all private institutions in the State in the range of twenty to twenty-five million may occur by 1970-71. . . . the estimate does not include an additional burden of deferred maintenance and physical plant which is estimated today at a combined total of forty-five to fifty-five million. If funded over a five-year period the annual cost would be approximately nine to eleven million dollars." From the *Report of the Select Committee on the Future of Private and Independent Higher Education in New York State/1968: New York State and Private Higher Education* (Albany: State Education Bureau, 1968), p. 17.

1830 or to Burlington Railroad President Charles Elliot Perkins in 1887, when he snapped at sentimentalists for putting into people's heads the notion that the world owes everybody a living: "The managers of the railroad property have no right to spend money belonging to the corporation from simply charitable motives."[34]

The transfer from a *personal* to a *corporate* response to the fate of private education was undertaken in the early 1950's when Frank Abrams of Standard Oil Company (New Jersey), Irving Olds of United States Steel Corporation, and Alfred Sloan of General Motors Corporation began to argue that the corporation could not remain indifferent to important needs of the larger society. Posed was a challenge to the traditional theory of the firm which viewed the business enterprise as a profit-maximizing entity exclusively. The practical result of these efforts was the historic *A. P. Smith v. Barlow* case, in which the legal barriers to corporate giving were cut away.[35] The defendant was a New Jersey concern, the A. P. Smith Manufacturing Company, which incurred a stockholder's suit by making a grant of $1,500 from general operating funds to Princeton University. Judge J. C. Stein opened the doors to a more active corporate role by declaring in his 1953 decision upholding the grant that there is nothing that "promotes the growth and service of the American university or college in respect of the matters here discussed that can possibly be anything short of direct benefit to every corporation in the land. The college that has trained men and women is a ready reservoir from which industry may draw to satisfy its needs for scientific or executive talent."*

* Five years later, corporate business extended the permissible legal reach of the business enterprise toward higher education by developing a test case in a regulated industry when the Union Pacific Railroad allocated $5,000 of company funds to the Union Pacific Railroad Foundation—a nonprofit foundation established by the company. See Clarence C. Walton, "The Changing Face of a Business Corporation's Responsibilities," *Temple University Economic and Business Bulletin,* XVII, September, 1964, pp. 4-14.

Regrettably, the exciting first steps taken by Messrs. Abrams, Olds, and Sloan have had a rather dreary sequel. Support has not increased when compared to profits. And it is in the light of this relatively ineffective performance by corporations toward institutions of higher learning that David's summons takes on a particular relevance. "Instead of a fraction of 1 per cent of profits which they are now providing, business must increase its contributions [to higher education] closer to the 5 per cent the tax laws allow." Business must invest more in the intellectual resources these institutions can provide, says David, for "the world needs the guidance and wisdom that the best of business and the best of the academic community, working together, can provide."

If complacency had been the tone of the founders' remarks, one statement of David's would have done much to dispel it. In cataloging the ills of our troubled era, he says:

> Fearful wars in our neighborhoods, an unpopular war halfway around the world, crime, a vicious cycle of life on welfare for millions, delinquency, racial tensions, dreadful urban congestion, violence to humanity and to nature—these and other issues that disturb us deeply all have their roots in the unprecedented rate of change that man has unleashed. None of us can say that business leadership is doing enough to meet these problems.

The capstone of the proceedings is perhaps to be found in observations made by Harry Scherman, who says, in effect: Yes, the American economy has been a success beyond our most sanguine expectations. Within a few years the gross national product, measured in constant dollars, will pass the trillion mark—"a situation fairly describable as a material utopia." But is this sufficient unto the aspirations and the needs of human beings? With his final remark, Scherman implies that it is not: "I should not be surprised if that income-utopia presents us with even more worries than those we now have."

The points made by both David and Scherman were recently put very forcefully, if with perhaps some exaggeration, by the editor of *The Economist* in a special survey of the United States entitled "The Neurotic Trillionaire":

> The United States in this last third of the twentieth century is the place where man's long economic problem is ending, but where his social problems still gape. On any rational view, the enormous fact of that approach to economic consummation should rivet all attention. It is almost certainly the most momentous news-story so far in the history of the world. But people in the United States are at present wracked by the stretching to snapping point of too many of their temporary social tensions, so that this society which represents man's greatest secular achievement sometimes seems to be on the edge of a national nervous breakdown.[36]

Some Critical Gaps

This brings us to a consideration of several major omissions in the CED founders' discussions. The first is an absence of any critical examination of the primary ethical or value issue in economics today—that is, the question of power. Historically social ethics involved analyses of injustices related to the startling contrasts between poverty and wealth; the issues were related to decent wages and to standards of living that denied minimum decencies to the masses and opportunity for advancement. The founders tend to cast their discussions within the historic frameworks—probably because the issue of distribution and consumption is still not fully resolved.

If, however, our productive capacities continue to improve at the rates we have become accustomed to—as Scherman and others are confident will happen—then it is only a matter of time until the issue of power will occupy the position of centrality in social and business ethics. "Black power," "student power," "community power" are but the first manifestations of what will become the central ideological issue business leadership will soon have to face. There remains in business a tendency to view the power issue in terms of property when, as a matter of fact, the propertyless are showing increasingly innovative ways to assert their own powers.

How does one deal, for example, with demands on business made by black leadership for allocation of corporate resources—without acceptance of the normal channels of accountability to those who provide such resources? Do private universities—which desperately need financial support from the private sector if they are to remain private—belong almost exclusively to faculty and students? If so, what are the implications for business from whose ranks were recruited trustees? Will private enterprise lose power because of widely accepted predictions that the business firms will no longer be the major source of innovation?

A very concrete and immediate issue that finds no place in the founders' discussions is that concerning a redistribution of income through some such device as the negative income tax or the guaranteed annual wage, whereby those now living in poverty on the fringes of the labor market could move into the economic mainstream. The single reference to such proposals, which are now assuming an increasingly high priority in the American dialogue, comes from Ralph Flanders, who dismisses the matter by asserting that "to finance a permanent caste of paupers [through the negative income tax] is un-American."

Yet more and more people are assuming that poverty can be alleviated through federal budgetary policy. One of the first and most widely quoted negative income tax proposals was made five years ago by Professor Milton Friedman of the University of Chicago,[37] and other prominent negative income tax proposals have been offered by Robert Lampman, Robert Theobald, and James Tobin.[38] Furthermore, on the eve of the last Presidential election, the Ripon Society, representing an influential group of Republicans, endorsed the negative income tax on the premise that such a tax, properly administered, would provide economic security for all the nation's poor in a manner not calculated to demean the recipients, as well as provide incentives for economic self-betterment.[39] The CED itself actively discussed guaranteed income as an alternative to the present welfare system at a New York "Policy Forum" in May, 1968. Additionally, in the spring of 1969, CED's Research and Policy Committee authorized the creation of a subcommittee on poverty and the welfare system, which will examine among other issues "how the public assistance system should be modified, or whether it should be replaced by a new program of income maintenance." The debate is sharpening, and it is difficult to believe that before long this debate will not bring about a vastly improved—and more human—system of "welfare" that will encourage incentive without exposing the less-privileged to the hazards of an open marketplace in which they are unequipped to compete.

This is to suggest that the range of inquiry, while far reaching by normal standards, did not go far enough when judged by the criteria of today's crises. The business vision of the future seems less daring and multidimensional, for example, than that offered by Herman Kahn, Anthony Wiener, Daniel Bell, Eugene Rostow, and others of the American Academy's Commission for the Year 2000. Kahn and Wiener have developed tables that seek to identify the characteristics of society as we pass into the twenty-first century.[40] They list the following fifteen characteristics of the coming "post-industrial" or "post-mass-consumption society":

1. Per capita income about fifty times the preindustrial
2. Most "economic" activities are tertiary and quaternary (service-oriented), rather than primary or secondary (production-oriented)
3. Business firms no longer the major source of innovation
4. There may be more "consentives" (vs. "marketives")
5. Effective floor on income and welfare
6. Efficiency no longer primary
7. Market plays diminished role compared to public sector and "social accounts"
8. Widespread "cybernation"

9. "Small world"
10 Typical "doubling time" between three and thirty years
11. Learning society
12. Rapid improvement in educational institutions and techniques
13. Erosion (in middle class) of work-oriented, achievement-oriented, advancement-oriented values
14. Erosion of "national interest" values
15. Sensate, secular, humanist, perhaps self-indulgent criteria become central

An appropriate rejoinder to this criticism would remind us that preoccupation with the domestic power problem and with the features of the world in the year 2000 possess an *avant garde* quality; the businessman should not be so "far ahead" that he becomes "far out." The point is well taken. Yet even if it were disallowed, it is certainly fair to suggest that the collective experiences and judgments of the founders demonstrate, without question, that from the ranks of business will emerge—to recall the words of K. T. Keller—more "dangerous" men. If a willingness to challenge the status quo and a desire to induce change or hallmarks of "dangerous" men, then the entrepreneurial and innovative businessman will always be dangerous.

PART THREE

Redefining Corporate Purpose: A Historical Perspective

10. The Three Eras of American Business

CLARENCE C. WALTON

Because pre-Civil War America had received such a deep impress from its prevailing rural tradition and its experience with small and locally-operated businesses, it is possible to consider the first century of the country's existence as one unified period. To be sure, while continuous change was evident the moment the industrial revolution began to take hold in this country, it was the dramatic social and industrial development following the Civil War that greatly accelerated the pace of change. Increasingly the older ideology, grounded in European theological and philosophic developments of the sixteenth century and nurtured by the rural and mercantile style of the earlier America, had to contend with new realities—the factory in place of the farm, an ascendancy of the machine over the tool, the necessity for professional managers to succeed the "family" administrative team. Nevertheless, such was the impress of the earlier experiences and traditions that viewpoints were slow to change, and a new rationale for business responsibility and leadership was even slower to develop.

Hence a certain arbitrariness must inevitably attend efforts to identify that moment in the post-bellum period when a new approach to business mores can be said to have emerged, or to pinpoint precisely when the ideology shifted from the view of business responsibility as a *personal obligation* to the present view of *corporate response*. For purposes of discussion, three periods have been identified to bracket three modes of thought regarding the nature of responsibility. The first, which may be called the Era of the "Business Man" (with appropriate emphasis to underscore its personal, individualistic nature) ran roughly from 1860 to 1890; the second was the Era of the Business System, ending about 1940; and the third, the Era of Corporate Enterprise, is still with us and will continue into an indefinite future.

Era of the "Business Man": 1860-1890

In a real sense the American intellectual quality was profoundly influenced by three European high priests: John Calvin (1509–64), John Locke (1632–1704), and Adam Smith (1723–90). Calvin provided a theology which could justify the businessman; Locke laid the theoretical bases for property in the political system; and Smith provided the apologia for a business order. The early Christian tradition was marked by skepticism toward anyone engaged in commerce, and there was little to choose between Aquinas and Luther on this score. Calvin was the first major leader in religion to accept as valid the motivational basis for the individual businessman in frugality, hard work, and perseverance by justifying it in terms of possible signs of God's blessings. Locke's views of property provided the key element for structuring representative government when he argued that men must be protected in the possession and use of their private property. And Smith provided the impersonal discipline of market competition in a profit-and-loss mechanism to shore up those who might, as individuals, drift from Calvin's stern precepts. One notes, in passing, how the new apologetics justified the individual entrepreneur *and* the business system: to be involved righteously in the world's work was to be engaged meaningfully in God's work.

Here was the conceptual seed-ground for the Yankee-Protestant tradition. Ours was a middle-class morality which insisted that Adam Smith's brand of economic competition existed not only to increase the wealth of the nation but to strengthen individual character as well; it stressed, according to Locke, the primacy of *opportunity* rather than of equality so that men of ability could prove themselves and reap the rewards of their own efforts. Finally, the ideology insisted that government had a solemn obligation to maintain a sound moral climate for all its citizenry. The Yankee-Protestant tradition, profoundly conservative, was built around the virtues of rural life, small towns, small businesses, and individualism.[41]

What cannot be missed in the early American creed is the constant reiteration that the economic system must perform as a moral agent to elicit the best from men. In this context, the notion of responsibility found expression among businessmen who accepted success as the natural reward of superior moral character because—with a nod toward Calvinist morality—they also accepted *personal* obligations toward the poor and less fortunate. Young women recruited to textile mills lived in strictly supervised boarding houses; liquor was banned in most towns; schools and colleges were supported in New England and in the West; southern slave owners found every motive—"except that it was personally profitable"[42]—to justify the slave system. The harshly repressive attitude of New England textile owners toward the female employee—not too different from the slaveowners' attitude toward Negro slaves—too often characterized the all-pervasive paternalism of the new republic. Nonetheless the obligations of the patron were widely accepted by the rising mercantile elite.

Views did change in the post-bellum period, but slowly. "Bigness" in either the public or private sector continued to be viewed with instinctive suspicion; the impersonality implicit in corporate bureaucracy was disdained; the unneighborliness of urban living was condemned. The stage was set for the glorification of the self-made man, of the Andrew Carnegie variety, and for increasing hostility toward the corporate *system* as the dominant role passed from individual entrepreneur to organization archons.

At the risk of oversimplification, it is tempting to think that Abbé Felix Klein, a French visitor to these shores at the turn of the century, distilled the essential flavor of "business responsibility" as defined in the 1860–90 period when he wrote: "to make money is only half the task; the other half is to use it well."[43] The clergyman then indicated how use of surplus wealth might appropriately proceed. Basically there were only three patterns: (1) a wealthy businessman might leave his fortune to offspring—but this was both selfish and unwise because great legacies are often squandered by children; (2) he could create a foundation—but this turns over management of the estate to others and transforms individual charity into impersonal philanthropy; or (3) he could personally make donations during his lifetime. That the third alternative appealed most to Abbé Klein is indicative of the period's basic philosophy; namely, that personal ability to acquire should be coupled with a capacity to dispose wisely: this became the quintessence of business responsibility! The individual entrepreneur was the acclaimed hero because he represented to a remarkable degree the virtues of industry and farsightedness so much esteemed in the early ideological strain.

Era of the Business System: 1890-1940

A dilemma was created by the transformation of the economy—from one dominated by individual businessmen to a system run by professionals who control an interlocking business system. According to the Anglo-Saxon tradition of law, a business enterprise existed exclusively to make profits and to distribute them equitably to stockholders; this legalism provided large firms of this period with justification for not venturing boldly into areas unrelated to business. Yet the very size of organizations such as the Standard Oil Company and United States Steel Corporation, the impersonality of corporate bureaucracies, and the concentration of power over markets and over people combined to create a state of great uneasiness. There was fear that the businessman of the new breed was rising to power because of his organizational (*sic* manipulative) skills and not because of his entrepreneurial qualities; there was concern that the conscientious small entrepreneur was in danger of being ground down by the conscienceless corporation. Thus the system came under attack not because it was inefficient but because it allegedy debased the moral quality of the country.

And what constituted this moral fibre? The answer emphasized qualities of self-reliance, freedom of action, opportunity for risk-taking—the very virtues of a bygone Jeffersonian era. Indeed, the country remained in the grip of what Alfred Kazin has once described as a "half-nostalgia for a pre-industrial society."[44] With societal expectations so ambiguous, if not contradictory, it is not surprising that the meaning of social responsibilities was difficult for the business community to grasp.

The country obviously placed a high premium on efficiency, and on smallness: if therefore efficiency required great size then efficiency would have to be sacrificed. Justice Peckham made that proposition clear in 1897 when he ruled that in conflict situations involving protection of the small businessman versus economic efficiency, the small businessman came first. A few years later, in an 1899 speech to the Chicago Conference on Trusts, William Jennings Bryan thundered: "There is no good monopoly in private hands!" Time and again this profound concern for the interests of small enterprise threatened by industrial giants was expressed in court opinions.

Big business over-reacted, basing its case on the argument that increased productivity on its part constituted the most realistic measure of its responsibilities. This view was pressed with such vigor that when the American Society of Mechanical Engineers sought in 1908 to develop a code of social responsibilities, it was felt that business support could be secured only on the crassest basis. One scholar noted that "even such innovations as better ventilation and lighting in the shops had to be presented, not primarily as humanitarian measures, but in terms of the higher productivity and efficiency that would result."[45]

What general conclusion can be made for the period running from 1890 to the Great Depression? Certainly the country witnessed a sharp dialectic between two opposed schools. One insisted that size was inherently evil because the economic order's moral function was best served through competition among small businessmen. The other held that giant corporations were magnificently discharging their responsibilities because they generated an ever-increasing supply of goods and services for more and more people. There began to emerge finally a doctrine which held that business responsibilities were met when two conditions obtained: (1) when the industrial system provided *results* and (2) when the motives of those who ran the system were "high-minded." When Henry Ford died in 1947, observes Sigmund Diamond of Columbia University:

> Editorial opinion was virtually unanimous in holding not only that the consequences of his acts were of widespread public benefit, but that consideration of public service was the compelling motive which dictated his acts and decisions. One of the cardinal principles of classical economics was, of course, the compatibility of private striving and public welfare. But the two had been linked in such a way that the latter depended on the former. In the economic theory of the newspaper editors, there was no place for explicit avowal of private striving. *Service had replaced profit as a basic category of entrepreneurial motivation* [Italics added].[46]

But the postwar period brought an acceleration of firms' growth, and the question now was to determine whether the service motive could be incorporated into the corporation's basic goals by executives who, unlike Ford, did not own what they managed.

Era of Corporate Enterprise: 1940-

Throughout the 1930's, big business was on the defensive in a manner never before experienced. The depression shattered confidence in big business claims that its productive efficiencies were beyond challenge. Heretofore size was bad because it threatened another's freedom: now it was bad because it was disfunctional. It was not then very clear and is only now becoming evident, that "market power" attributable to size had little effect on instability in the economy because instability is fundamentally the product of fiscal and monetary policies of big government.

When the shadows of a second world war spread ominously over the global landscape there was a sense of foreboding that the American industrial machine would prove incapable of turning out the sinews of war in quantities capable of blunting the totalitarian threat. Largely through the efforts of big business, a brilliant production record was achieved. And when a predicted postwar depression failed to materialize, when the peacetime gross national product hit record highs, when technology offered opportunities for newcomers to launch science-related industries, a shift in public opinion became discernible.

By the early 1950's polls and studies conducted by Elmo Roper and by the Survey Research Center of the University of Michigan revealed a lingering but dwindling fear of corporate size and an overwhelming vote of confidence in business' capacity to produce.[47] It was the popular view that the trend toward ever-enlarging organization had been blunted so that the future would probably—and rightly—bring some diminution in relative size. This general lay attitude has been reinforced by testimony from experts in the academic community, who have suggested that industrialism requires a system of organization based on many large-scale industries as the dominant method of production. One report noted that "Such a system cannot be an atomistic one with infinite fractionalization of power and distribution of decision making. Authority must be concentrated. . . . Authority may be concentrated in a monistic or pluralistic arrangement. *It is our view that the dominant arrangement will be pluralistic. Where there is one locus of power, there will come to be several; where there are many, there will come to be fewer.*" [Italics added].[48]

Perhaps the most pithy and most perceptive comments on the changed view toward business has been expressed by Richard Hofstadter in these words: "Once the United States had an antitrust movement without antitrust prosecutions; in our time there have been antitrust prosecutions without an antitrust movement."[49] In this new setting, corporate leadership became psychologically ready for new challenges.

Increasingly today the corporation, *qua* corporation, is viewed not simply as a profit-maximizing instrument but as an agency whose resources should be employed for many missions only tangentially related to profits. The steady enlargement of business' role suggests that the profit ethic—so revolutionary during the eighteenth century and so commonplace in the nineteenth—may now have become a reactionary relic of times irrevocably lost. It does not follow, of course, that business responsibilities will mean abandonment of the profit motive; nor does it mean that business will go galloping off to perform all kinds of good works.

The long and the short of it is simply this: business responsibilities will no longer be measured exclusively by criteria appropriate to performance within a purely economic-technical system. The social system consists of many sub-systems, each with its own dynamic and particularized rules. Yet each sub-system is influenced by the other, as is illustrated in the medieval and the American colonial experiences, when religious thought profoundly affected the economies—Catholicism in the first instance and

Calvinism in the second. When the systems interact frequently, influences from one to the other may flow quickly and cause important changes on the receptors as well as on the initiating system itself.

Breaching the walls of traditional economic theory has made many businessmen and many economists uncomfortable. Relatively few people seem concerned to find a systematic explanation for the way in which American capitalism has operated in fact; rather they have been more preoccupied in offering explanations of how it was supposed to operate in theory.[50] Yet we sit on the edge of a new day as idol after idol in the American mythology has been toppled by events; casualties include the ethos of the farm and the small town, the old apotheosis of the *petit entrepreneur*, the enshrinement of pure competition and profit-maximizing theories. It has become painfully evident that events are outdistancing theory and that the large corporation is responding in imaginative and innovative ways to spur the market toward greater social progress. It is not without significance that some former critics of big business have turned in new directions of approval—as witness men such as Adolph Berle, Jr.,[51] and David Lilienthal.[52]

From an original emphasis on the primacy of owner-interests, businessmen have moved to embrace a broader community of claimants—possibly because of the imperatives of the Sherman and Clayton acts and the pressures of public opinion. More recently large enterprise has shown a willingness to venture voluntarily into "nonbusiness" arenas because of a growing inner conviction that great resources should be directed toward great social purposes. But why has this occurred?

Some steps in this evolutionary development are readily explained. Stockholders today are less investors than they are depositors;[53] owners do not really assume the obligations that historically were attached to property; the Ricardian theory of workers as merely mechanistic factors of production has given way long since to a view of employees as creative human beings who must be respected; corporations voluntarily are introducing due process for middle managers unprotected by unions.[54] But there are other more subtle—as well as more arresting—developments, as witness the growing concern with the *quality* of American life. It might even be suggested that the definition of "consumer" is being significantly enlarged from one stressing a share in goods and services to the measure of a man's pocketbook to one emphasizing a share in the good life to the measure of a man's personality.

Two central questions remain to be answered. (1) How can the great corporation graduate into the more challenging role of furthering progress toward a great civilization? (2) How can this enlarged function be articulated through an appropriate managerial apologetic that makes sense to stockholders and to society at large?

Toward an Integrated System

Business leaders—young and old—are seeking to refashion such an apologetic. The effort is being undertaken precisely at that point in history when the institutions that normally provide for social integration, as well as opportunities for personal identification, are themselves in disarray and are losing their respective identities. In many respects, therefore, the business community itself is being asked to provide elements for integration. The integrated system deals with such things as identity, legitimacy, status, community, respect, and dignity—as these are all features that are profoundly related to the quality of modern life. But the market system has historically insisted on a quid-pro-quo relationship, and an exchange economy seems inadequate to meet the challenge for integration. As Kenneth Boulding has observed:

> The trouble with the corporation and indeed with almost all purely economic organizations is that everybody has good terms of trade with them. We do ask what General Motors can do for us and the answer is, "Quite a lot." If we are employed

by it, it gives us good wages; if we buy from it, it gives us automobiles. As a result, however, of existing in a purely exchange environment it creates a weak integrative system. One of the problems of General Motors is that nobody loves it much, hence it is ultimately vulnerable to shifts in the integrative system which would deny its legitimacy. The only answer to this seems to be a system of reciprocity which combines the virtues of the exchange system, which are very great, with the development of an integrative structure.[55]

What seems to be occurring is that the two institutions with the greatest power—government and business—are being asked to provide innovative social instruments that can integrate an apparently disintegrating society. The government has vast powers through its taxing capacity and through its control over money and credit by the Federal Reserve System. These powers represent the heart of federal influence over the economic system. The corporations, too, have vast powers. Of the roughly 1.2 million private corporations about 600 carry out about 80 per cent of the basic business operations; it is this small handful of companies to which the American people are looking for help at a moment of national and international transformations.

The appeal for help is coming largely from people representing the minorities long denied a role in the production-exchange system. Persistent neglect has had the predictable consequences; it has atrophied the will to work and the capacity for participation in the competitive system. We employ the words "hardcore" to describe this group and business approaches the problems of employing the hardcore rather gingerly. Clearly corporate leadership doubts whether any quid pro quo can be realistically achieved within the short term. But it should be noted that the criterion for determination of important corporate policy has been "the exchange" mechanism. Now business is being asked whether this criterion is truly adequate and whether reciprocity (gain for each but not necessarily in equal proportions) is not also required.

The willingness to move beyond the pure exchange system into a reciprocal system may not prove as difficult as business expects. The history of corporate behavior is apposite at this point. An industrial society is always viewed as achievement-based. It is, in point of fact, quite reciprocal in nature. Few managers and few workers are fired for incompetence; leadership in both management and unions often goes to great lengths to protect the less adept. Sociologist William Goode of Columbia University has offered a persuasive thesis to the effect that our industrial achievement-oriented society protects the inept simply because "rigorous application of the norm of performance to the actions of all members of a collectivity would, under most circumstances, destroy both its social structure and its productivity."[56]

What William Stolk has called the corporation's "public business" may turn out to be the primary instrument which allows business the opportunity to share in the creation of an integrative system. Participation in this work does not mean the abandonment of the principle of self-interest or destruction of the profit motive. But Stolk and others in the CED forums have insisted that the corporation must look beyond profit to recognize the principle of reciprocity. Theodore C. Sorensen, former special counsel to Presidents Kennedy and Johnson, wrote to this point in the following terms:

> The question is whether that is enough of a motive and enough of a contribution? Is self-interest, no matter how enlightened it may be, ever enough? Is a corporation to engage in public activities only when it can find economic benefits? I think there are higher obligations, broader motivations. I believe that almost imperceptively the modern corporation has evolved into a social as well as an economic institution.
>
> Without losing sight of its need to make a profit, today's corporation has concerns and ideals and responsibilities which go far beyond the profit motive.
>
> The corporation's influence upon our country has power for good and for progress whether exercised or not; it imposes

> upon each corporation an obligation of leadership and citizenship which it has no choice but to accept. We do not say that a man who takes no interest in public affairs is a man who minds his own business. We say that he has no business being here at all.[57]

In a speech to the Association of National Advertisers on October 31, 1968, C. W. Cook, Chairman of General Foods Corporation, stressed the same idea. American business must be concerned with the social problems of our times, observed Cook, because involvement is "in our own best interest to make our American system work better and more equitably; involvement because business bears the obligation of leadership; and, most importantly, involvement because *it is right.*" Apropos here is the warning given by Edward E. Booher, Chairman of the Board of McGraw-Hill Book Company. "While the American industrial machine is one of man's greatest creations," says Booher, "its future depends less on this proven capacity and more on its ability to reach outward to meet the problems posed by big city ghettos and by minority needs for assimilation into the society." Because these are cancers in the heart and soul of America, Booher predicts that business "will in the decade ahead involve itself deeply with these issues. If it does not, we will be in for some radical changes."[58]

How involvement should occur is a matter of some debate. John W. Gardner, head of the Urban Coalition, has suggested that business must be involved but always as a business engaged in the production and selling of goods and services, and in providing equal opportunities for employment and education. When it becomes a matter of community leadership, Gardner prefers businessmen to act as individuals rather than as members of a corporation. There is a persuasive appeal to this position because it frees the businessman himself to "be his own man."

Yet individual participation is difficult when there are no officially recognized corporate incentives for participation. An enterprise normally demands the highest levels of energies and dedications from those engaged in its directions and leaves precious little time for individual participation in community affairs. *The Wall Street Journal* was not far off the mark when it reported that "the corporation is taking the place of the other woman in the so-called eternal triangle—and the staggering impact on executive marriages suggests that big business is the most demanding mistress of all."[59]

That such an organizational commitment takes precedence over the individual commitment is suggested by results of a study undertaken by John Mee of Indiana University. Mee's study is an attempted audit of representative opinion of holders of Master of Business Administration degrees toward their understanding and participation—and their companies' understanding and participation—in community affairs. Only one of six junior executives reported that his own corporation viewed community activity as being "very important" to the corporation—a finding that led businessman Charles Lazarus to conclude: "[Among other things the answers suggest] that most of our big business enterprises are ignoring most of the problems on the community front."[60]

It is heartening to note that every participant in the CED symposium is convinced that business must banish this neglect of social problems. At the level of middle-management are evidences of sharp differences on how participation should occur. Some would hold government to a rule-making and referee role only and would insist that business should engage in public works only where a profit can be realized. But there are others (and a greater consistency is evident in the commentaries of most of the senior executives) who ask that the corporations redefine purposes that will go beyond profitability. In a challenging way, therefore, some senior executives appear more venturesome than their junior colleagues.

The debate is far from ended. Its ultimate resolution will more likely be hammered out on the anvil of practical application of policy to concrete problems. Some businesses will undoubtedly seek to develop a "table of public needs" and then seek to match these public needs to the particular resources of the enterprise itself. Some will wish to have their business join in a consortium designed to achieve maximum impact (housing, jobs, education, and health care in a coordinated building program). Other businesses will find their contributions to social problems best realized through a compact with a government agency. Clearly no large enterprise can afford the luxury of indifference toward contemporary problems. This is the essential message which is shared through the CED. If problems faced by business are large so, too, must be the corporate vision.

Notes

1. B. J. LOISBY, "Management Economics and the Theory of the Firm," *Journal of Industrial Economics,* XV (July, 1967), 165-76.
2. See RICHARD EELLS, *The Meaning of Modern Business* (New York: Columbia University Press, 1960); and the interpretation given in F. X. SUTTON, *et al., The American Business Creed* (New York: Schocken Books, 1962), esp. pp. 57-61.
3. THEODORE LEVITT, "The Gap Is Not Technological," *The Public Interest,* XII (Summer, 1968), 122.
4. PHILIP H. ABELSON, "The Inexorable Exponential," *Science,* CLXII (October 11, 1968), 221, Copyright 1968 by the American Association for the Advancement of Science.
5. BARBARA WARD, "The International Setting," in Clarence C. Walton, ed., *Today's Changing Society* (New York: Institute of Life Insurance, 1967), pp. 129-30.
6. J. STANFORD SMITH in the Introduction to, "Beauty and the Business Community," *The General Electric Forum,* VIII (October-December, 1965), 22.
7. THOMAS A. PETIT, *The Moral Crisis in Management* (New York: McGraw-Hill Book Company, 1967).
8. A. A. BERLE, JR., *The Twentieth Century Capitalist Revolution* (New York: Harcourt, Brace & World, Inc., 1954), p. 168.
9. FRITZ STERN, "The Historical Setting of Student Unrest," In *The Background of Student Unrest,* Columbia College Alumni Association, New York, 1966, pp. 4-5.
10. GEORGE STEINER, *Government's Role in Economic Life* (New York: McGraw-Hill Book Company, 1953). Professor Steiner preferred the words "mixed economy" because they best indicated the three important features of modern life. The three relate to the fact (1) that economic activity is shaped by a blend of private and public economic decisions; (2) that appropriate roles for government control and private initiative must be delineated; and, (3) that there is a middle way between extremes represented by laissez-faire and complete government control. (p. 236).
11. RENSIS LIKERT, *The Human Organization: Its Management and Value* (New York: McGraw-Hill Book Company, 1967), p. 258.
12. *Proceedings of the Super Market Institute Midwinter Conference, January 7-10, 1968* (Chicago: Super Market Institute, 1968), p. 16.
13. L. W. MOORE, "Whose Problem Is It?," *Social Service Outlook,* III (April, 1968), 2.
14. ROBERT LILLEY, "Heroless Drama Ahead," *The MBA,* December, 1967, p. 16.

15. LANGSTON HUGHES, "Warning," from *The Panther and the Lash* (New York: Alfred A. Knopf, Inc., 1969). © Copyright 1967 by Arna Bontemps and George Houston Bass. Reprinted by permission of Alfred A. Knopf, Inc.
16. BEN B. SELIGMAN, *Permanent Poverty: An American Syndrome* (Chicago: Quadrangle Books, 1968).
17. THORSTEIN VEBLEN, "The Engineers and the Price System," in Max Lerner, ed., *The Portable Veblen* (New York: The Viking Press, 1921 [Reprinted in Robert Lekachman, ed., *The Varieties of Economics* (Vol. II: New York: Meridian Books, World Publishing Co., 1962), p. 121.]
18. See MICHAEL HARRINGTON, *Toward a Democratic Left* (New York: The Macmillan Company, 1967).
19. LAWRENCE A. CREMIN, *The Genius of American Education* (New York: Random House, 1966), p. 31.
20. MARCIA FREEDMAN, "Business and Education," in Ivar Berg, ed., *The Business of America* (New York: Harcourt, Brace & World, Inc., 1968), p. 367.
21. JAMES B. CONANT, *Comprehensive High School: A Second Report to Interested Citizens* (New York: McGraw-Hill Book Company, 1967).
22. LIKERT, *op. cit.*
23. WILLIAM BENTON, "The Economics of a Free Society: A Declaration of American Economic Policy," *Fortune,* XXX (October, 1944). CED reprinted this article as its Supplementary Paper No. 1.
24. KARL SCHRIFTGIESSER, *Business Comes of Age: The Impact of the Committee for Economic Development, 1942-1960* (New York: Harper & Brothers, 1960), p. 68.
25. *The New York Times*, July 13, 1967.
26. *Paying for Better Public Schools,* a Statement on National Policy by the Research and Policy Committee of the Committee for Economic Development, New York, 1959; and *Raising Low Incomes Through Improved Education,* a Statement on National Policy by the Research and Policy Committee of the Committee for Economic Development, New York, 1965.
27. WILLIAM E. LEUCHTENBURG, *The Perils of Prosperity: 1914-1932* (Chicago: University of Chicago Press, 1958), p. 249. © 1958 by The University of Chicago.
28. ROBERT L. HEILBRONER, "The View from the Top: Reflections on a Changing Business Ideology," in Earl F. Cheit, *The Business Establishment* (New York: John Wiley & Sons, Inc., 1964).
29. KARL SCHRIFTGIESSER, *Business and Public Policy: The Role of the*

Committee for Economic Development: 1942-1967 (Englewood Cliffs, N. J.: Prentice-Hall, Inc., 1967), p. 1.

30. SUTTON, *et al., op. cit.,* p. 217.
31. SCHRIFTGIESSER, *Business and Public Policy, op. cit.,* p. 15.
32. VICTOR R. FUCHS, "Redefining Poverty," *The Public Interest,* VIII (Summer, 1967), 89.
33. DANIEL P. MOYNIHAN, "We Need Three Things," *Social Service Outlook,* III (March, 1968), 3.
34. CLARENCE C. WALTON, *Corporate Social Responsibilities* (Belmont, Calif.; Wadsworth Publishing Company, 1967), p. 57.
35. *A. P. Smith Manufacturing Company v. Barlow, et al.* (May 19, 1953), New Jersey Supreme Court (Chancery Division), *Atlantic Reporter,* 1957, pp. 188-89.
36. NORMAN MACRAE, "The Neurotic Trillionaire: A Survey of Mr. Nixon's America," *The Economist,* a supplement, May 10, 1969, p. 11.
37. MILTON FRIEDMAN, *Capitalism and Freedom* (Chicago: University of Chicago Press, 1962), Chapter 12.
38. ROBERT J. LAMPMAN, "Prognosis for Poverty," in *Proceedings of the Fifty-Seventh Annual Conference of the National Tax Association,* 1964, pp. 71-81, and his "Approaches to the Reduction of Poverty," *Papers and Proceedings, American Economic Review,* LV (May, 1965), 521-29; ROBERT THEOBALD, *Free Men and Free Markets* (New York: C. N. Potter, 1963); JAMES TOBIN, "On Improving the Economic Status of the Negro," *Daedalus,* 94 (Fall, 1965), 889-95; and JAMES TOBIN, JOSEPH PECHMAN, and PETER MIESZKOWSKI, "Is a Negative Income Tax Practical?," *Yale Law Journal,* November, 1967, pp. 1-27.
39. *Ripon Forum,* IV (August, 1968), 21-24.
40. HERMAN KAHN and ANTHONY WIENER, *The Year Two Thousand: A Framework for Speculation of the Next Thirty-Five Years* (New York: Macmillan Company, 1967), p. 25. See also the Summer, 1967, issue of *Daedalus* devoted to the topic, "Toward the Year Two Thousand."
41. RICHARD HOFSTADTER, *The Age of Reform* (New York: Alfred A. Knopf, Inc., 1961), pp. 8-9.
42. ALFRED H. CONRAD and JOHN R. MEYER, "The Economics of Slavery in the Ante-Bellum South," *Journal of Political Economy,* LXVI (April, 1958), 95.
43. OSCAR HANDLIN, *This Was America* (Cambridge: Harvard University Press, 1949), pp. 412-13.
44. ALFRED KAZIN, *On Native Ground: An Interpretation of Modern American Prose* (New York: Harcourt, Brace & World, Inc., 1942), p. 11.

45. MONTE CALVERT, *The Mechanical Engineer in America: 1830-1910* (Baltimore, Md.: The Johns Hopkins University Press, 1967), p. 270.
46. SIGMUND DIAMOND, *The Reputation of the American Businessman* (Cambridge: Harvard University Press, 1955), p. 153.
47. BARTON R. FISHER and STEPHEN B. WITHEY, *Big Business as the People See It* (Ann Arbor, Mich.: University of Michigan Survey Research Center, 1951). A national sample of 1,227 adults showed continuing concern over power but satisfaction with results. See also ELMO ROPER, "The Public Looks at Business," *Harvard Business Review,* XXVII (March, 1949), 165-75; and JOHN D. GLOVER, *The Attack on Big Business,* Division of Research, Harvard Graduate School of Business Administration, Cambridge, Mass., 1954.
48. CLARK KERR, JOHN T. DUNLOP, FREDERICK HARBISON, and CHARLES A. MYERS, *Industrialism and Industrial Man: The Problems of Labor and Management in Economic Growth* (Cambridge, Mass.: Harvard University Press, 1960), pp. 289-90.
49. RICHARD HOFSTADTER, "What Happened to the Anti-Trust Movement?," in Earl Cheit, ed., *The Business Establishment, op. cit.,* p. 114.
50. ROBERT L. HEILBRONER, 'Capitalism Without Tears," *The New York Review of Books,* VII (June 29, 1967), 16.
51. BERLE, *op. cit.*
52. DAVID LILIENTHAL, *Big Business: A New Era* (New York: Harper & Brothers, 1953).
53. DOW VOTAW, "The Mythology of Corporations," *California Management Review,* IV (Spring, 1962), 58-73.
54. STEPHEN R. MICHAELS, "Industrial Due Process in Conflict Resolution at the Management Level" (Doctoral thesis, Columbia University, New York, 1967).
55. KENNETH BOULDING, "Technology and the Integrative System," in Walton, *Today's Changing Society, op. cit.,* p. 65.
56. WILLIAM GOODE, "The Protection of the Inept," *American Sociological Review,* XXXII (February, 1967), 14.
57. THEODORE C. SORENSEN, "Corporate Leadership in the Public Arena," *Public Relations Journal,* XXIV (January, 1968), 28-29. (Copyright January, 1968, reprinted by permission.)
58. EDWARD E. BOOHER, "The Decade Ahead from a Publisher's View," *Science,* CLVII (November 17, 1967), 882-83.
59. *The Wall Street Journal,* May 9, 1967.
60. CHARLES LAZARUS, "Wanted: A New Breed of Business Leader," in *A Call to Action,* Beta Gamma Signa Business Fraternity, 1968, p. 29.

The Contributors

WILLIAM BENTON, one of CED's founders and its first Vice Chairman, is Chairman and Publisher of Encyclopaedia Britannica, Incorporated. A co-founder (at age 29) of the Benton & Bowles advertising agency, he started a second career in 1937 as Vice President of the University of Chicago. He became Assistant Secretary of State for Public Affairs in 1945 and served as U.S. Senator from Connecticut from 1949 to 1953. Benton has been U.S. Ambassador to the United Nations Educational, Scientific and Cultural Organization since 1963 and is the author of articles and books, including *This Is The Challenge.*

DONALD C. BURNHAM became the eighth President and Chief Executive Officer of Westinghouse Electric Corporation in 1963. He began his career with General Motors Corporation in 1936 and joined Westinghouse in 1954, where he was Group Vice President before assuming his present post. Burnham is a member of the Business Council, of the President's Commission on Income Maintenance Programs, and of the Board of Incorporators of the National Corporation for Housing Partnership. He has been a CED Trustee since 1965.

EMILIO G. COLLADO has filled important policy-making posts in government and business. From 1938 to 1946 he held various positions at the Department of State in the field of international economics and finance, during the last two years serving as Director of the Office of Financial and Development Policy and Deputy to the Assistant Secretary for Economic Affairs. Collado was U.S. Executive Director of the World Bank in 1946-47, then joined Standard Oil Company (New Jersey) where he became Treasurer in 1954 and is now Executive Vice President and a Director. A CED Trustee since 1957, he was made Chairman of the Research and Policy Committee in 1966.

JAMES B. CONANT was President of Harvard University for twenty years (1933-1953) and has written more than a dozen books, including *The American High School Today* and *Modern Science and Modern Man*. During World War II, he served as Chairman of the National Defense Research Committee and Deputy Director of the Office of Scientific Research and Development. In 1953 he became U.S. High Commissioner for West Germany and two years later became U.S. Ambassador to that country. His service as a CED Trustee began in 1952.

DONALD K. DAVID was a member of the original CED Research Committee and from 1957 to 1962 was Chairman of the Board. He began his career as an instructor at the Harvard Graduate School of Business Administration, but left the academic world in 1927 for business. He served as President of the Royal Baking Powder Company and of American Maize Products Company. In 1942, he returned to the Harvard Business School and was for thirteen years its Dean. From 1956 to 1966 he was Vice Chairman of the Board of The Ford Foundation. He is a Director of several major corporations and a member of the Business Council.

WILLIAM H. DOUGHERTY, JR. joined the North Carolina National Bank in Charlotte in 1967 and is now Executive Vice President of the NCNB Corporation, a one-bank holding company. Dougherty received his bachelor's degree in business administration from the University of Pittsburgh in 1952, and after serving two years with the Air Force, he worked for Price Waterhouse & Company and for the Western Pennsylvania National Bank. He is a former Mayor of Liberty Borough, McKeesport, Pennsylvania.

RALPH E. FLANDERS was President of the Jones & Lamson Machine Tool Company in Vermont from 1933 to 1946. His government service began with membership on various government commissions and committees during the depression and World War II, and he was President of the Federal Reserve Bank of Boston from 1944 until 1946. Appointed U.S. Senator from Vermont in 1946, he was elected twice to full six-year terms. A member of the original CED Board of Trustees, Flanders was Chairman of its first Research Committee. He is the author of several books, ranging from technical works to *The American Century.*

MARION B. FOLSOM joined Eastman Kodak Company in 1914 and served as Treasurer from 1935 to 1953. His government service began with membership on the President's Advisory Council on Economic Security in 1934, and in the years since he has been a member of numerous government commissions and committees. Folsom became Under Secretary of the Treasury in 1953 and served as Secretary of Health, Education, and Welfare from 1955 to 1958. He was re-elected to the Board of Directors of Kodak in 1958, retiring in 1968. As a member of the original CED Board of Trustees, he was Chairman of the Field Development Committee. He was CED's Chairman from 1950 to 1953.

CLARENCE FRANCIS, a member of the original CED Board, was with General Foods Corporation from 1929 to 1958, serving as President, Chairman, and then as a Director and member of the Executive Committee. He was Chairman and Chief Executive Officer of Packard-Studebaker Corporation from 1961 to 1963. Francis was a member of various government committees during World War II, Chairman of the fund-raising campaign for the construction of New York's Lincoln Center for the Performing Arts, and the first President of the Economic Development Council of New York City.

PAUL G. HOFFMAN was the first Chairman of CED's Board of Trustees. Hoffman began his career in 1911 with the Studebaker Corporation and was its President from 1935 until 1948, when he was appointed the first Administrator of the Marshall Plan (ECA). He has been President of The Ford Foundation and a U.S. Delegate to the United Nations General Assembly. In 1959, Hoffman became Managing Director of the UN Special Fund and is now Administrator of the UN Development Program. He is the author of *World Without Want* and other books, as well as of many magazine articles.

HENRY G. HOHORST did his undergraduate work at the Massachusetts Institute of Technology and holds a master's degree in chemical engineering from the University of Colorado. He worked for Procter & Gamble Company and Monsanto Chemical Company, and in 1962 joined the New York Central Railroad as Manager of Chemical Industry Services, becoming Director of Operations for the merged Penn Central Railroad. Since 1968 he has been Director of Railroad Sales for ACF Industries Incorporated.

PHILIP M. KLUTZNICK, the developer of the Park Forest community in Illinois and now Chairman of the Board of the Urban Investment and Development Company, has devoted many years to public service. From 1933 to 1946 he held various posts in federal housing, including that of Commissioner of the Federal Housing Authority. He has served as a U.S. Delegate to the United Nations General Assembly and as U.S. Ambassador to the Economic and Social Council of the UN (1961-62), and he has been a member of numerous governmental committees. A CED Trustee since 1963, Klutznick is Vice Chairman for Education and Urban Development.

CHARLES MARSHALL has been Vice President of State Operations for the Illinois Bell Telephone Company since 1967. He received a bachelor's degree in agriculture from the University of Illinois in 1951 and served with the Air Force before joining Illinois Bell in 1953. He has served in various managerial and public relations positions both for Illinois Bell and the American Telephone and Telegraph Company. Marshall is a Trustee of Millikin University.

THOMAS B. MCCABE, after thirty-five years as President of the Scott Paper Company, became its Chairman and Chief Executive Officer in 1962 and now serves as Chairman of the Finance Committee. Among his various public posts, he has been Chairman of the Board of Governors of the Federal Reserve System from 1948 to 1951, following nine years' service as Chairman of the Board of the Federal Reserve Bank of Philadelphia. He was Chairman of the Business Advisory Council (now the Business Council) in 1944-45 and has been a Public Governor of the New York Stock Exchange. A founder of CED, McCabe was its Chairman in 1963-64.

RAYMON H. MULFORD is Chairman of the Board of Owens-Illinois, Incorporated, with which he has been associated for thirty-six years. He has served as Chairman of the Toledo Metropolitan Area of the National Alliance of Businessmen and as a Trustee of the National Industrial Conference Board. Mulford holds several corporate directorships and is a member of the Advisory Council of the Stanford University Graduate School of Business. Elected a Trustee of CED in 1964, he is Chairman of the Subcommittee on Business Structure and Performance.

ALFRED C. NEAL has been President of CED since 1956, prior to which he was First Vice President of the Federal Reserve Bank of Boston. He has served as Research Director for the Randall Commission and as a member of the President's Advisory Committee on Trade Negotiations. He is a member of the boards of the Council on Foreign Relations, the Education Development Center, and the Institute of Public Administration. Neal is author and co-author of several books and numerous articles.

JAMES A. NORTON is President of the Greater Cleveland Associated Foundation since 1962 and Director of the Cleveland Foundation. He has held numerous university teaching posts, including that of Professor of Area Development at Case Institute of Technology. He is President of the American Society for Public Administration. Norton was Chairman of the CED Area Development Advisory Board.

HARRY SCHERMAN was a founder of the Book-of-the-Month Club and has been Chairman of the Board since 1950. He is the author of several books, including *The Promises Men Live By: A New Approach to Economics*. He has served as President and Chairman of the Board of the National Bureau of Economic Research. Scherman joined the original CED Board in December, 1942, and was for many years a member of the Research and Policy Committee.

WILLIAM C. STOLK, the tenth Chairman of the Board of CED, started his business career as a timekeeper for American Can Company at the age of fifteen. He worked his way up through the sales side of the company, retiring in 1965 as Chairman and Chief Executive Officer. He continues as a Director of the American Can and other corporations and heads a management consulting firm, W. C. Stolk & Associates. A CED Trustee since 1951, Stolk chaired the twenty-fifth anniversary committee and was elected Chairman of the Board in 1968.

THOMAS A. VANDERSLICE holds a doctorate in physics and chemistry from the Catholic University of America. In 1956 he joined General Electric Company, first serving in the Missile and Space Vehicle Department and then in the Research Laboratory. He became General Manager of the company's Information Systems Sales and Service Division in 1968.

CLARENCE C. WALTON has been a teacher, consultant, and author in the fields of business history and corporate social responsibility. He has served on the faculties of Duquesne University and the Columbia Graduate School of Business. In 1964, he was appointed Dean of the Columbia School of General Studies, leaving that post in the fall of 1969 to become President of the Catholic University of America. A prolific author, his recent writings include *Corporate Social Responsibilities* and *Ethos and the Executive: Values in Business Decision-Making.*

ROBERT J. WESTON is General Manager of the Building Products Division of Boise Cascade Corporation in Boise, Idaho. Following service as a Captain in the Army Air Force during World War II, he received a bachelor's degree in English at the University of Oregon. He worked for firms in the wood products field, and for Packard Bell Electronics Corporation. From 1963 to 1966 Weston was Vice President of Marketing for Temple Industries.

FRAZAR B. WILDE, after 52 years with the Connecticut General Life Insurance Company, became Chairman Emeritus in 1966. Wilde has also been a consultant to the Board of Governors of the Federal Reserve System, Vice Chairman of the nonpartisan Business Committee for Tax Reduction, and a member of the Advisory Committee on International Monetary Arrangements. He served as Chairman of the CED Research and Policy Committee from 1953 to 1958 and then as Chairman of the Commission on Money and Credit. From 1964 to 1968, he was Chairman of the Board of CED.

W. WALTER WILLIAMS is Chairman of Continental, Incorporated, a mortgage banking, insurance, real estate, and property management firm. Active in Seattle civic affairs, he has also held principal offices with the Mortgage Bankers Association, the International Chamber of Commerce, and other organizations. He was national Chairman of Citizens for Eisenhower in the 1952 elections and saw government service as Under Secretary of Commerce from 1953 to 1958. A CED Trustee since 1946, Williams was Chairman of the Board from 1948 to 1950.

Index